The DRAWING BOOK

JOHN DEACON

AN ASHTON ORIGINAL

From Ashton Scholastic
Sydney Auckland New York Toronto London

CONTENTS

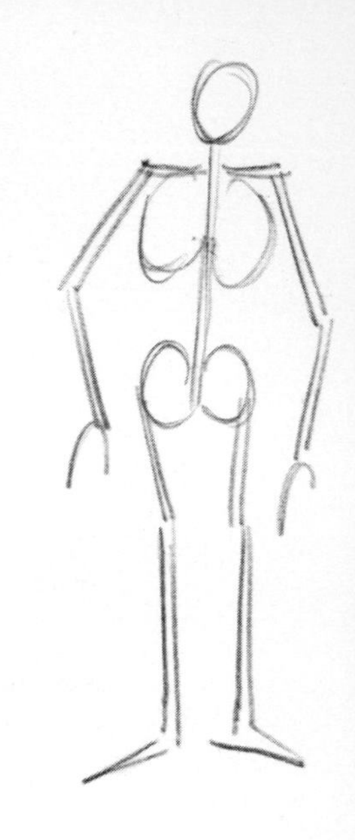

4 Introduction
5 Meet Your Guides
6 Squiggles
7 Transferring
8 Copying
9 Tracing
10 Relationship of Size
11 Size – Near and Far
12 Overlapping
14 Basic Shapes
15 Shapes & Roughs
16 Shadows
17 Shading
18 Convergence
19 Perspective
20 3D Effect
21 Materials & Style
22 Detail
23 Emphasis
24 Measuring & Observing
25 Composition
26 Techniques
27 Figures – Introduction
28 Figures – Proportions
29 Figures – Starting Points
30 Heads
31 Profiles
32 Faces
33 Portraits
34 Eyes, Mouth & Nose

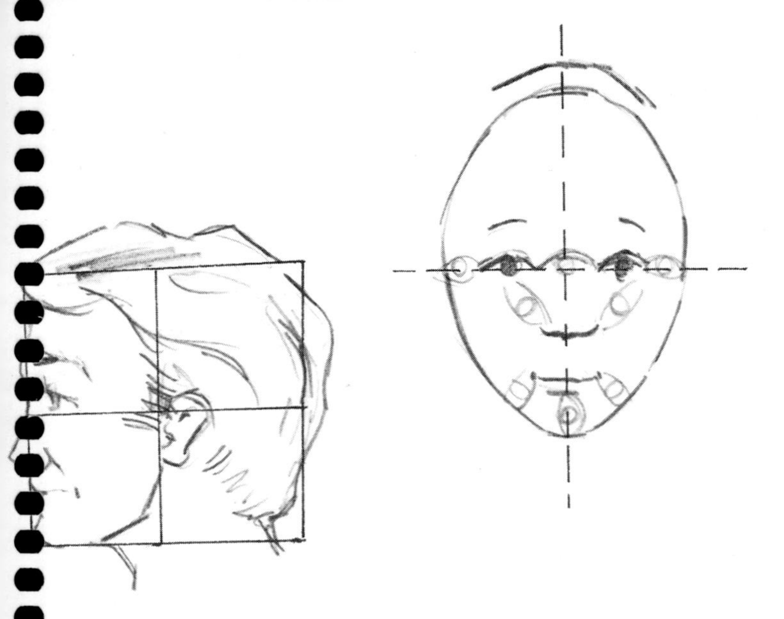

35 Nose & Hair
36 Expressions
37 Different Ages
38 The Hands
39 Feet & Shoes
40 Arms
41 Legs
42 Building the Figure
43 Positions
44 Situations
45 Groups
46 Clothing
47 Still Life
48 Animals
49 More Animals
50 Birds
51 Trees
52 Plants
53 Flowers
54 Landscapes
55 Buildings
56 Cars & Hot Rods
57 Trains, Buses & Trucks
58 Bikes & Boats
59 Planes & Rockets
60 Cartoons
61 Cartoons Again
62 Caricatures
63 Monsters & Other Things
64 Your Own Style — Imagination

INTRODUCTION

There is something magical about drawing.

The marks you place on the paper can change a blank space into a portrait of Grandma, a landscape including your secret

place, a detailed study of your left thumbnail – or they can tell a whole story of what, when, where and why things happened. Maybe your marks look like nothing special, but make you feel good while you do them or when you look at them later.

Drawing is a way of seeing –

Drawing is a way of storytelling –

Drawing is a way of having fun –

All magicians must practise hard so that others don't see the trick – so that an audience sees the magic only. Drawing requires the same kind of patience, and that takes time. Then people will ask 'How was that done?'

This book will show you many simple and easy tricks to improve your drawing, so that you draw what you see and get your story across to others.

BEGINNING TIPS

Always draw something special or particular rather than something general.

Always look at what you draw rather than draw from memory.

Don't worry about mistakes – they are part of the fun of drawing.

Now go and draw!

SQUIGGLES

When you squiggle or doodle, you're drawing. Allow your mind, as well as your line, to wander.

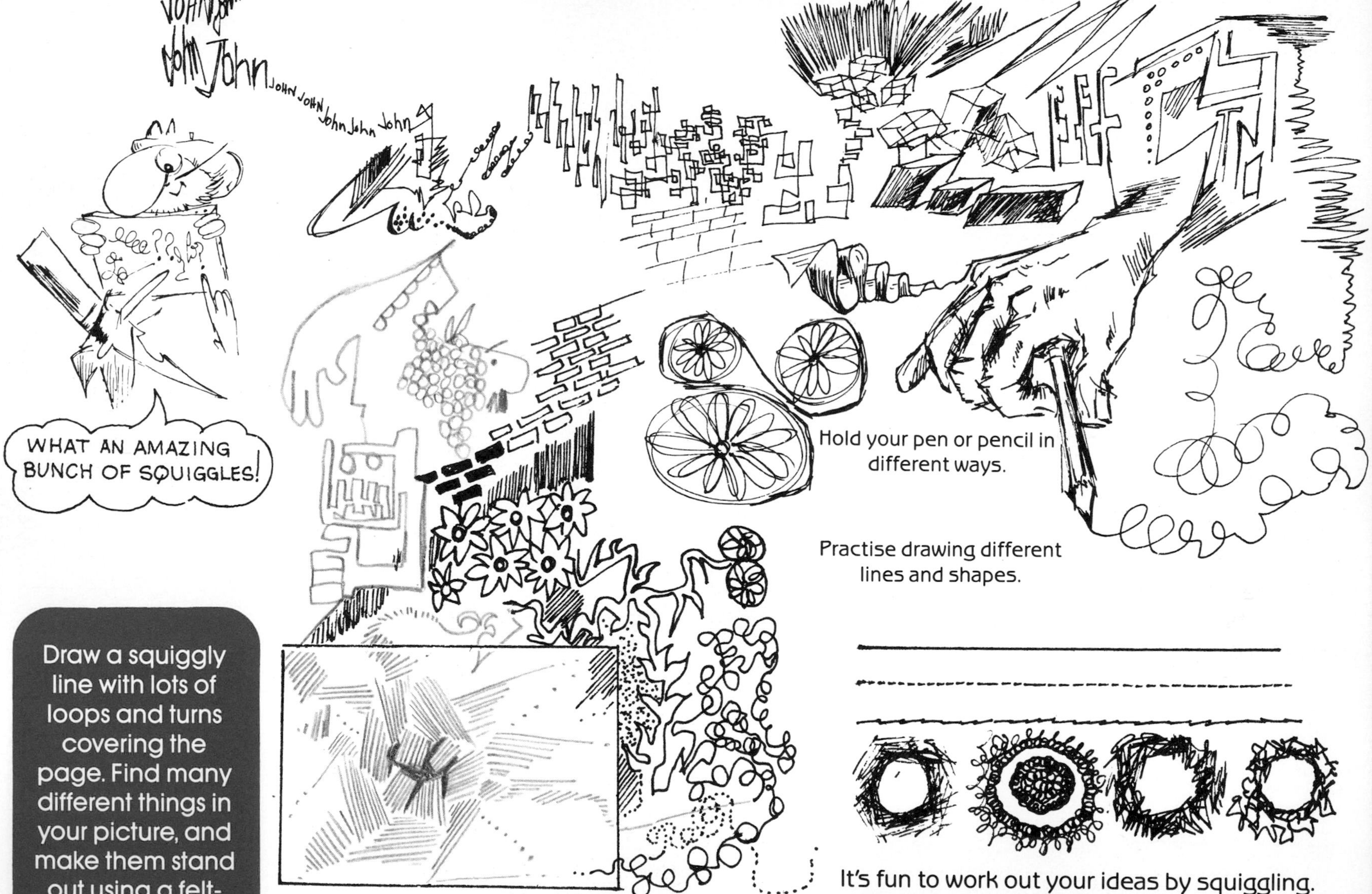

Hold your pen or pencil in different ways.

Practise drawing different lines and shapes.

Draw a squiggly line with lots of loops and turns covering the page. Find many different things in your picture, and make them stand out using a felt-tipped pen.

If your squiggling looks good, it may even become the finished job.

It's fun to work out your ideas by squiggling. Look for parts you like and bits you enjoyed doing, and make a full picture from them. To do this you need to copy carefully.

TRANSFERRING

Transferring is a method of copying more accurately and changing scale. With the help of a simple grid, you can copy any object and draw it to whatever size you wish. All the great masters learnt to draw by copying.

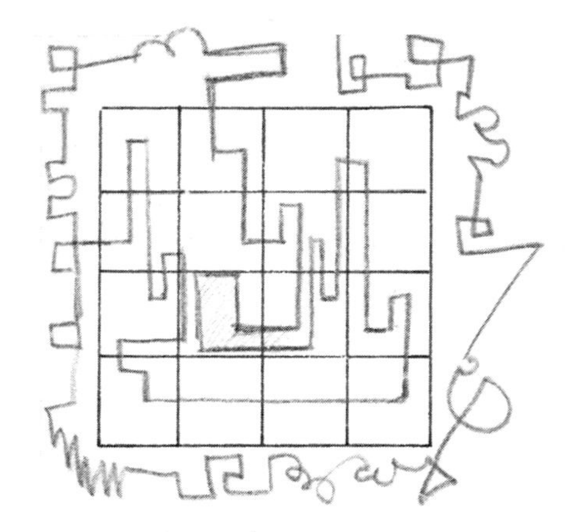

Draw a box around a part you like in your squiggle. Divide the box into equal parts. Then, on a plain sheet of paper, draw a box to whatever size you wish your finished job to be. Divide this box into the same number of equal parts. Now copy one square at a time to transfer your picture.

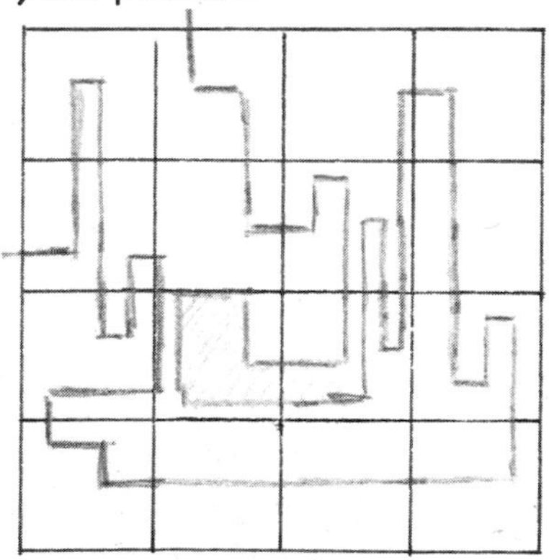

Using a felt-tipped pen, draw a grid of small squares onto a sheet of clear plastic (e.g. the lid of a shirt box). Place this clear grid over the picture you wish to copy. Next, divide your sheet of paper into the same number of squares. Now, with your grid, you can draw to your own scale by copying. This method teaches you to look very closely at what you are drawing.

Remember, draw only one square at a time. Notice how little there is in each square. Easy, eh!

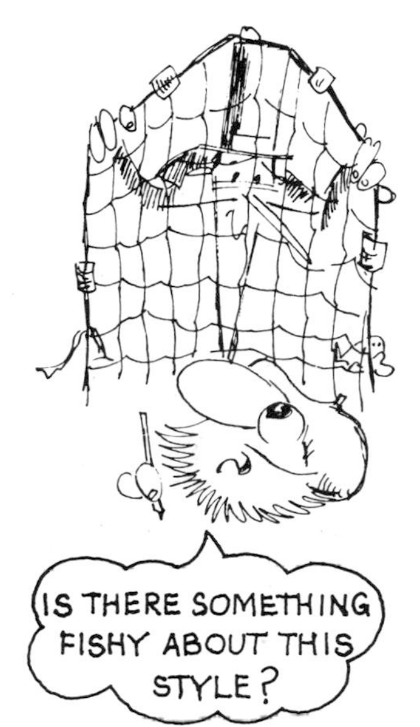

Make your squares distort a picture you wish to copy, by drawing your grid to different shapes.

COPYING

Copying is a good way to learn the importance of looking at the subject.

1. Make a frame from a piece of cardboard. Use this frame to surround what you're going to draw.

WHY DON'T YOU JUST TURN THE PAPER UPSIDE DOWN?

2. Now copy the space around the subject. Keep the spaces small by letting the frame cover parts of the subject.

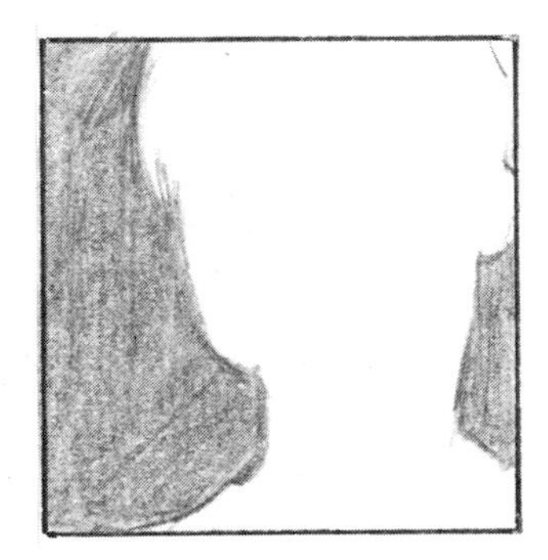

3. Now carefully look and fill in the detail.

Cut out a face or figure from a magazine. Cut it down the middle, and paste one half onto a large sheet of paper. Draw the other half, copying from the original.

To really use the skill of copying, turn an object upside down and then draw it.

This helps you copy what you *really* see — not simply what you expect to see.

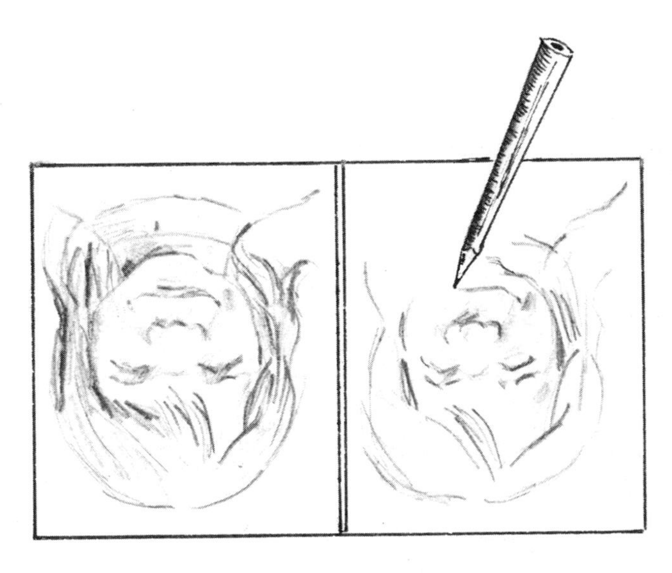

Don't forget that you can still copy unaided — doing what comes naturally!

TRACING

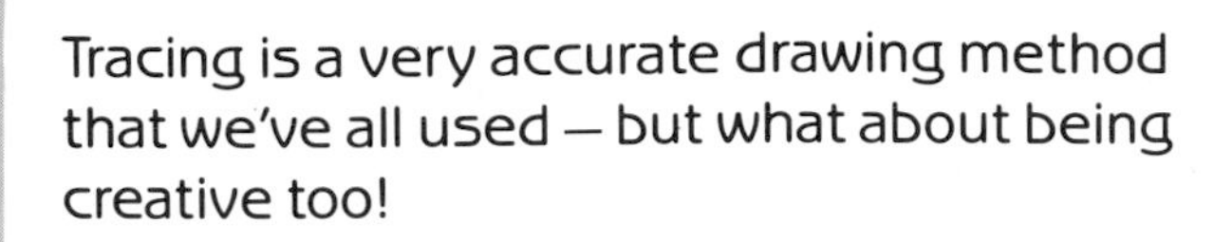

Tracing is a very accurate drawing method that we've all used – but what about being creative too!

Use tissue or any paper you can see the picture through.

Change faces and expressions.

Tracing paper overlays can be used to add lines and details to any picture you choose.

Simplify or add to your drawing.

Trace nature, using a piece of clear plastic.

If allowed, draw yourself on a mirror. Of course, you must be still!

How to transfer your tracing onto drawing paper.

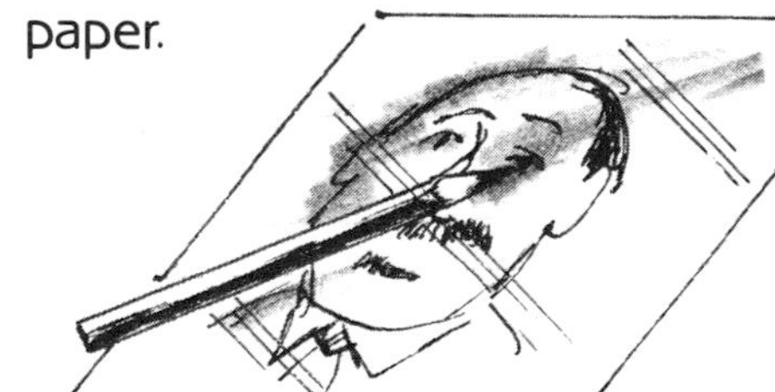

1. Shade the reverse side of your tracing.

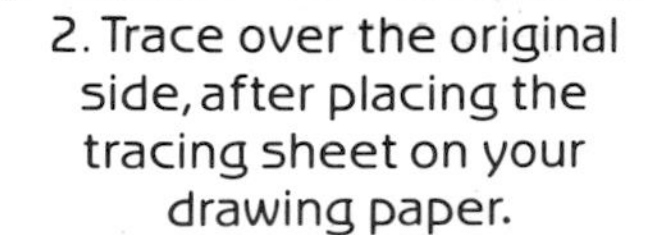

2. Trace over the original side, after placing the tracing sheet on your drawing paper.

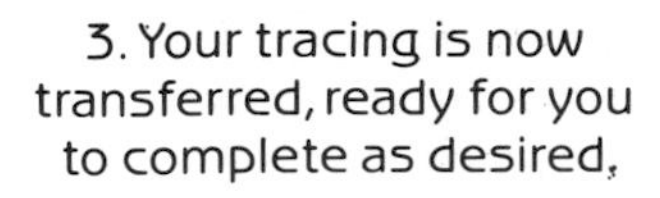

3. Your tracing is now transferred, ready for you to complete as desired,

Don't just read it. Get out and try it, now!

RELATIONSHIP OF SIZE

...BUT IN MY DRAWINGS I CAN CONTROL MY SIZE!

We tell the size of things in a drawing by putting something familiar near them.

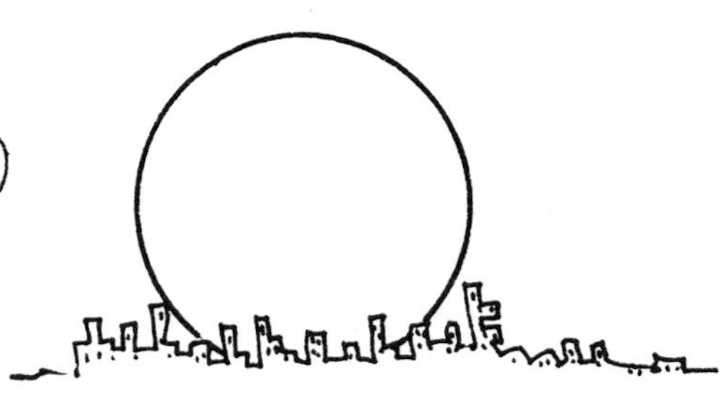

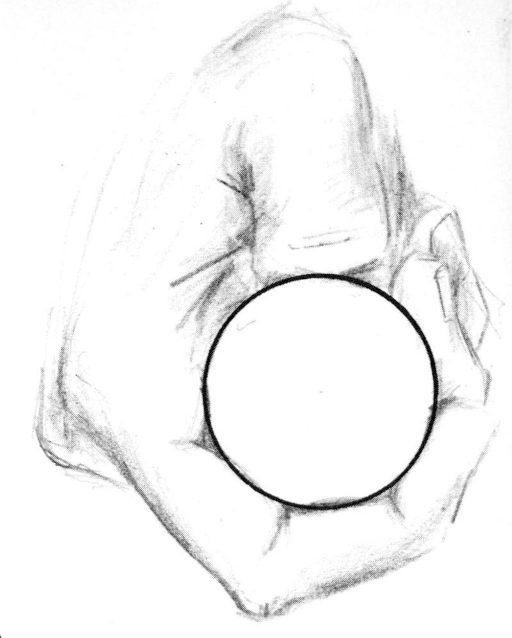

It's hard to realise, but all these circles are exactly the same size!

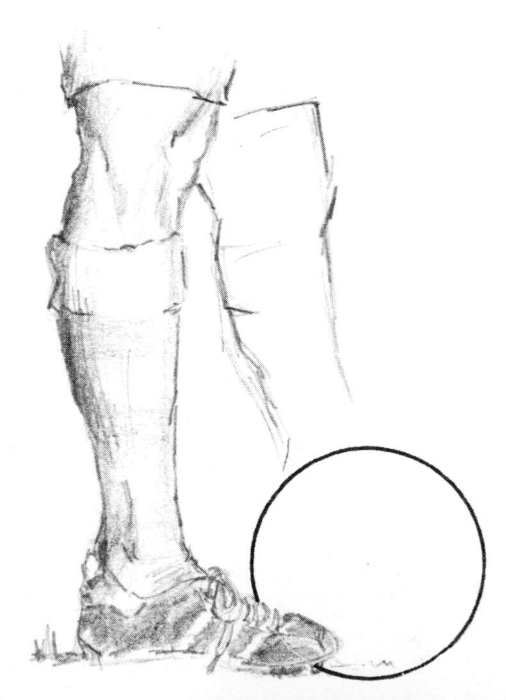

Draw a square. Now change its apparent size simply by drawing different objects next to it.

SIZE — NEAR AND FAR

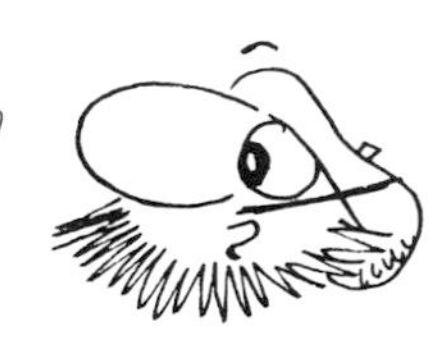

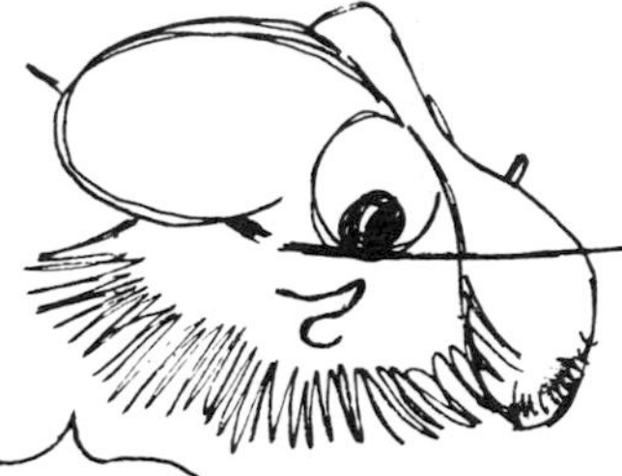

In drawings, the larger things are, the closer they appear.

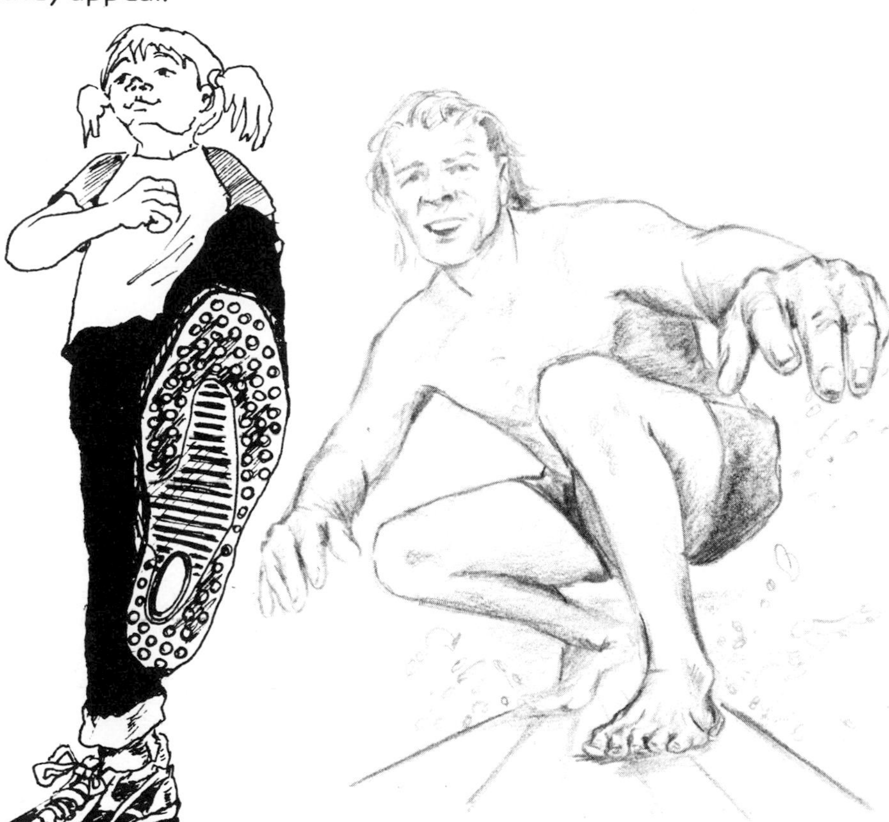

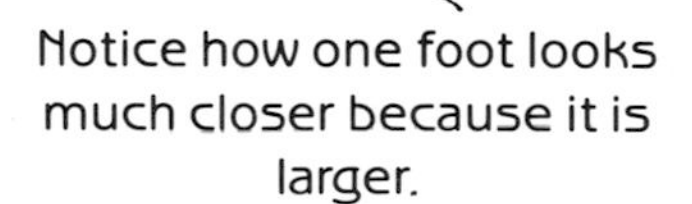

Notice how one foot looks much closer because it is larger.

Does the hand look closer to you than the foot?

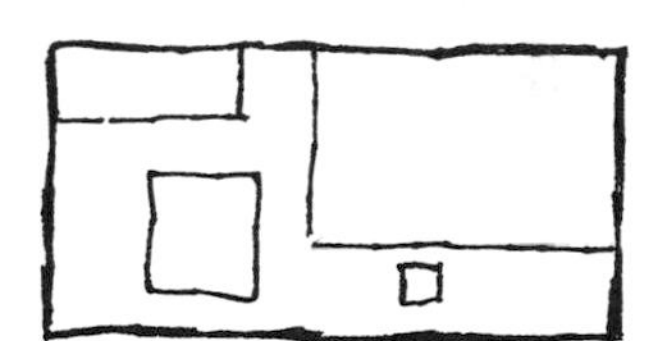

By playing with the size of shapes, we can make exciting designs that appear to show space and distance.

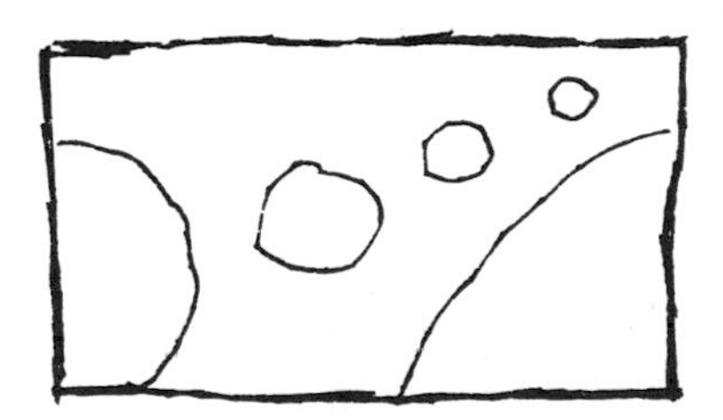

A looks closer than B because he is larger.

Copy one of the boxes above, and turn it into a picture.

Draw a boxer punching towards you. A big glove will help.

OVERLAPPING

Overlapping is when an object can be only partly seen because another object appears in front of it.

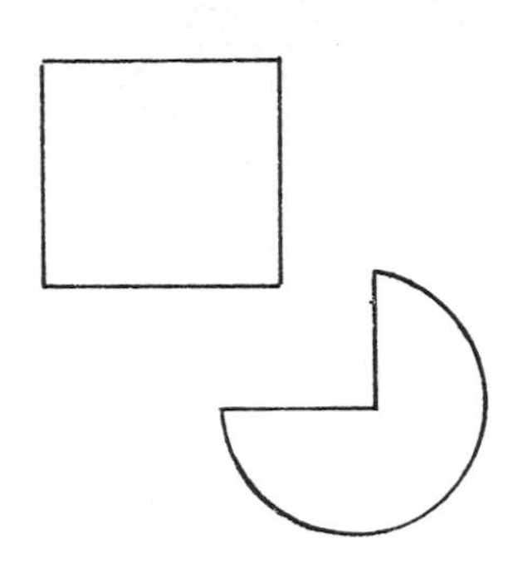

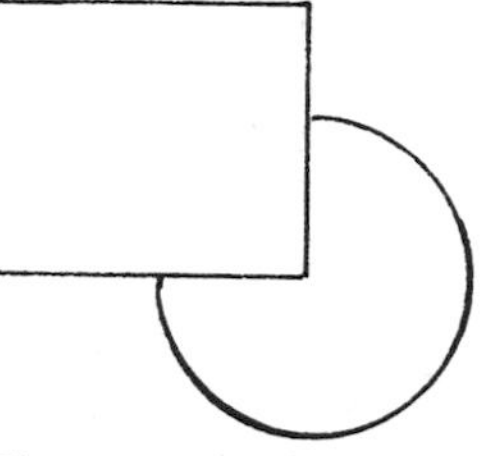

The square seems to be in front of the circle, because only part of the circle is drawn.

Overlapping makes all the objects in a picture seem to belong. They become one subject.

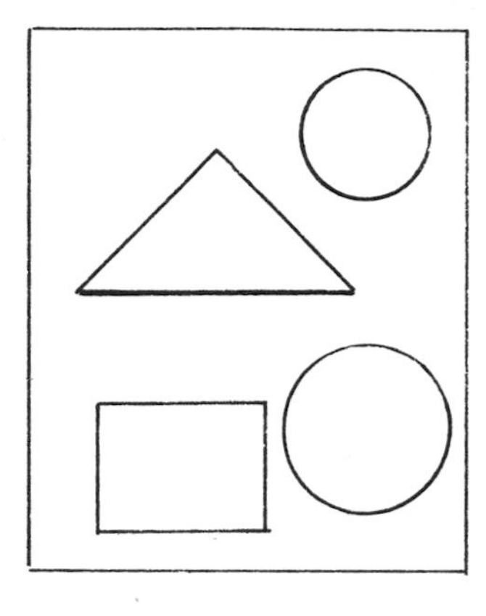

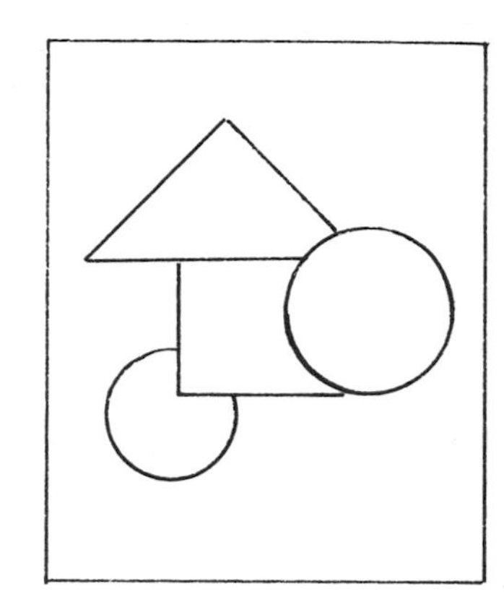

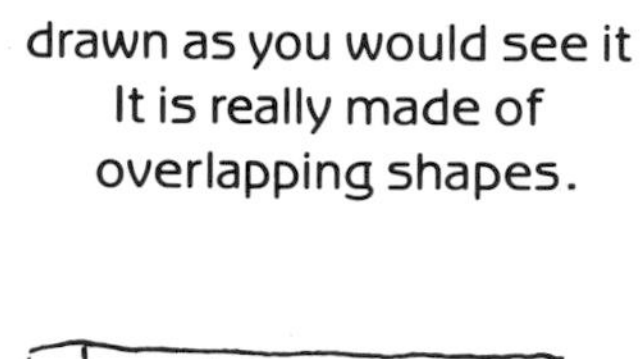

This room looks real because the furniture is drawn as you would see it It is really made of overlapping shapes.

Overlapping can show depth (distance). Remember, size helps too!

Draw a picture of the furniture in your room. First, draw the things you can see completely. Then draw the things you can only partly see.

OVERLAPPING

These overlapping rectangles show depth and movement. Our eyes tend to wander from the back to the front and so on.

While looking, we are actually guessing at what we cannot see. You too can add mystery by the simple trick of overlapping.

Draw a picture of a half-open box. Put something hiding in or behind it. You're now creating interest in what cannot be seen.

BASIC SHAPES

When sketching, look for shapes you know.

These common shapes become the basic forms or outlines of objects.

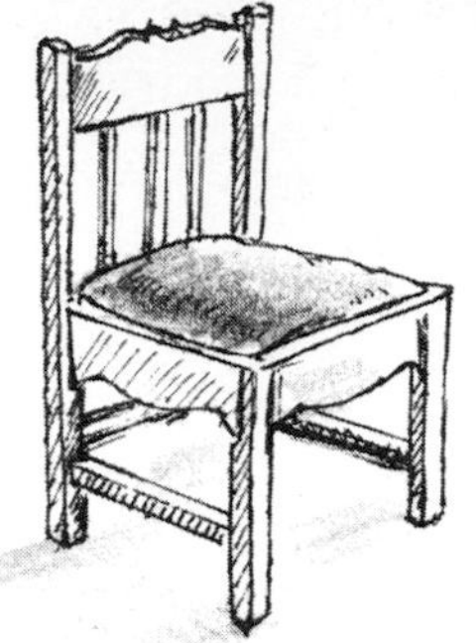

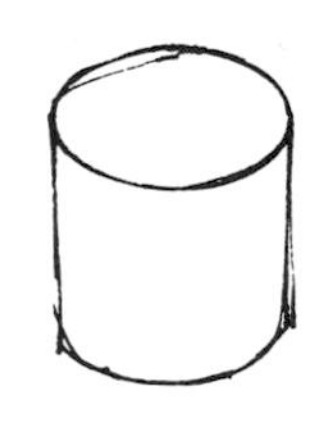

Most objects are made up of many different basic shapes.

Trace the basic shape of objects found in magazine photos. See how many basic shapes you can find.

SHAPES AND ROUGHS

All artists use some sort of skeleton to plan a drawing. This is generally called a rough. You can add to or take away from this.

Use light lines when sketching the shapes or roughs for a drawing. They are much easier to correct.

Find new shapes and ideas for starting points by shading or filling in the space *around* objects.

A horse or a mass of scribble? Such a sketch can help you work out how to draw the pose you want.

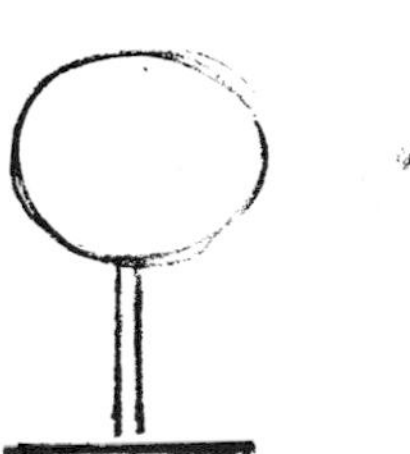

A simple start to a tree.

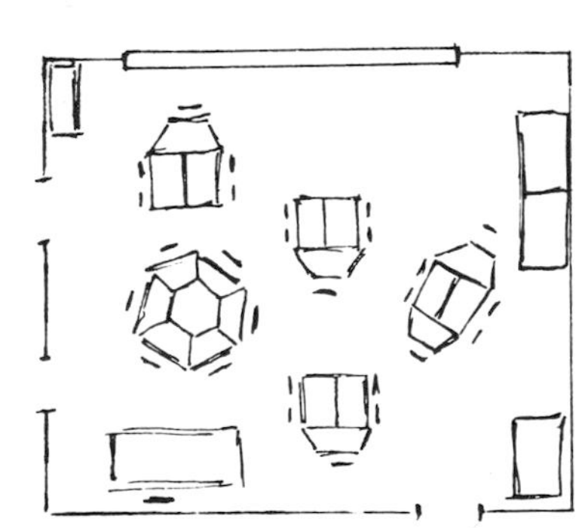

A good way to think in basic shapes is to draw a plan of a room.

Use simple, basic shapes to guide you when sketching roughs.

Draw 20 circles on a page. By adding a quick line or two, make 20 different things in 5 minutes. Try this again using other shapes.

SHADOWS

Shadows can help your picture look more real. Always look for the source of the light when you're drawing. Notice how a line drawn from the light source to the top of the object and then to the ground below will show the length of the shadow.

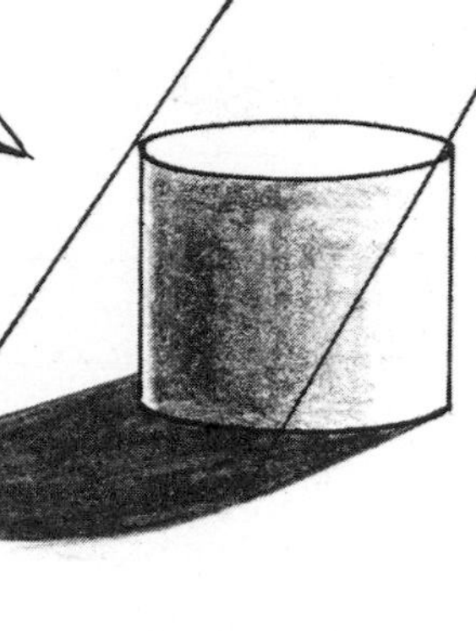

Don't forget, different shapes cast different shadows.

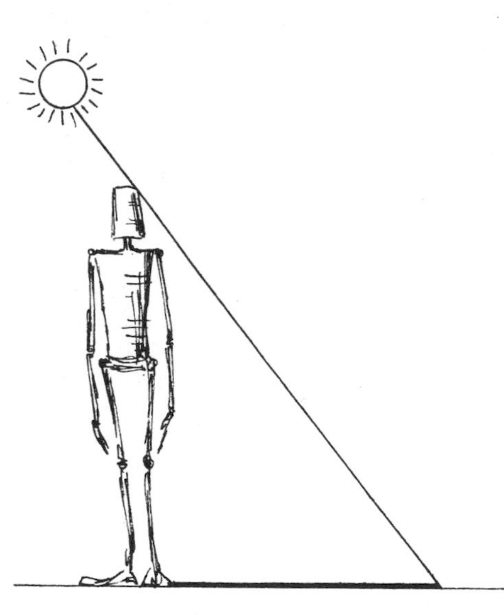

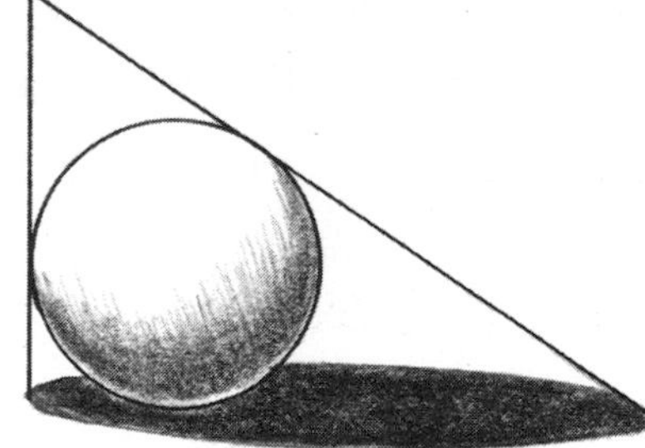

Use a strong light source to produce dark shadows on an object. Now draw the object in black and white only. Try the same with a face!

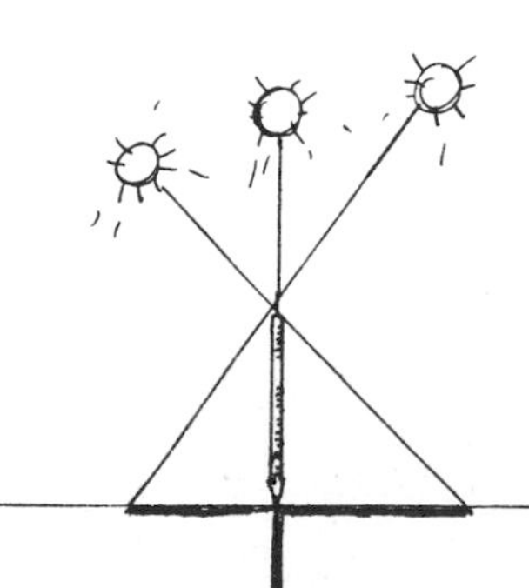

When the light source moves, so does the shadow.

What happens when the shadow hits the wall?

Remember, light occurs indoors too!

SHADING

An object not only casts a shadow, but also has shadow on it. This is shown by shading.

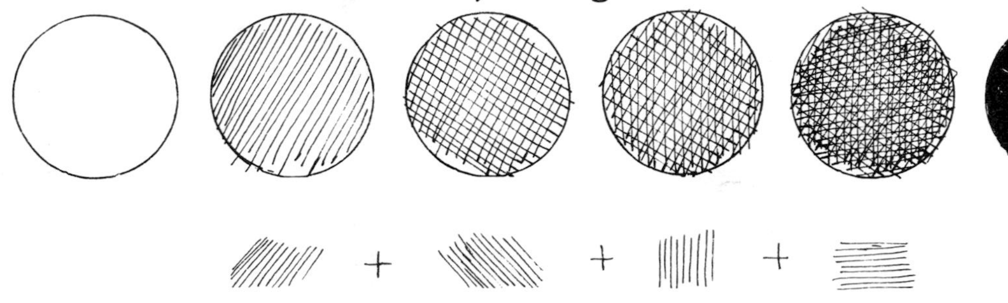

Shading can be simply done by using different directional lines.

CROSS HATCHING IS VERY USEFUL TOO!

Add shading until some areas are dark.

Experiment with different types of shading.

Experiment with different areas of shade for effect.

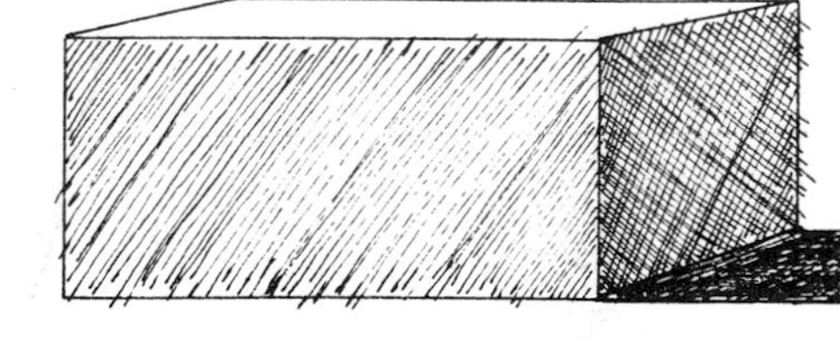

Four shades are enough to make this box look real.

Here the shading is divided into different degrees, to show the roundness of the object.

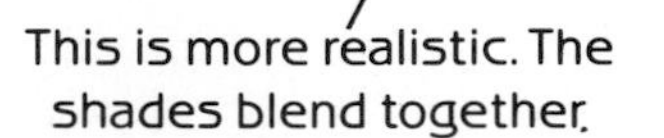

This is more realistic. The shades blend together.

Draw a table. Look closely at the shading, and then shade using the four degrees and black and white. Now try the same for a ball, a pencil and a face.

CONVERGENCE

All parallel lines appear to move away to a vanishing point. They converge (become closer) as they travel into the distance.

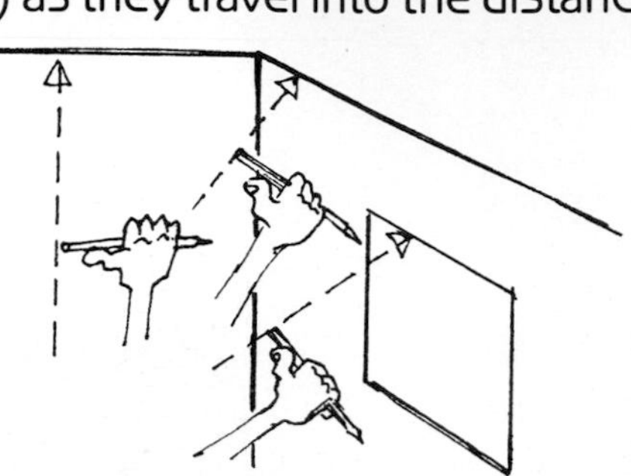

Use your pencil to judge levels and angles when drawing. Close one eye first to avoid double vision.

How you see things depends on where you stand.

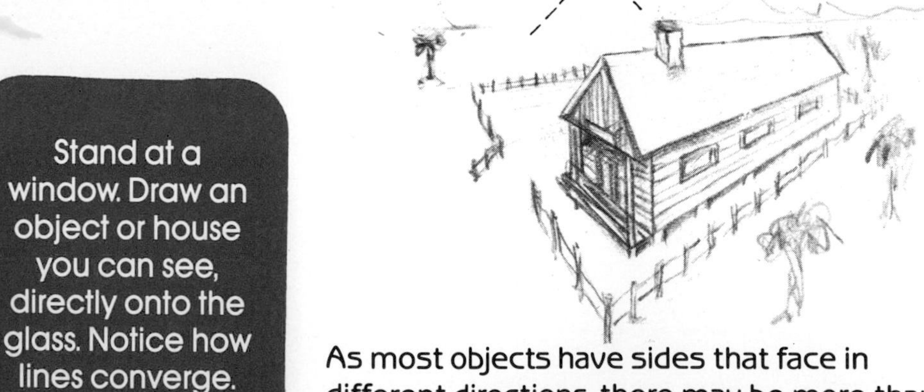

Stand at a window. Draw an object or house you can see, directly onto the glass. Notice how lines converge. Remember, close one eye.

As most objects have sides that face in different directions, there may be more than one vanishing point.

This can be important when drawing buildings, as most are simple box shapes.

Drawings will appear much more real and solid if you check lines of convergence.

PERSPECTIVE

We can give an impression of depth and distance by distorting (lines and size) towards a vanishing point.

vanishing point

horizon

spacing becomes closer towards the horizon

size becomes smaller towards the vanishing point

parallel lines converge towards the vanishing point

detail of objects is strong and distinct close to the viewer, but becomes indistinguishable as objects recede

Eye level is always at the horizon. Therefore, to draw this you're a giant or you're standing on a hill

Different viewpoints affect the perspective of your drawing.

SO THAT'S YOUR POINT OF VIEW!

Directly above table.

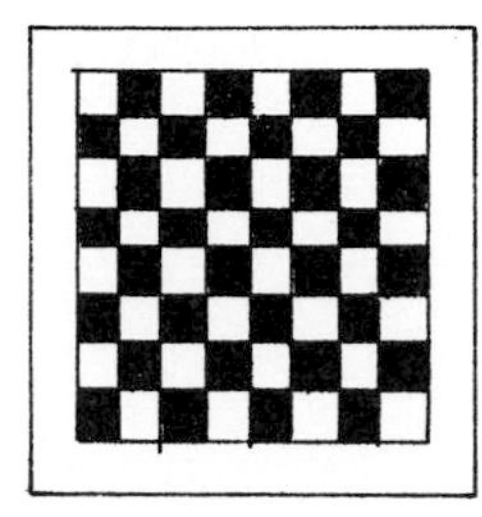

Standing near table looking down.

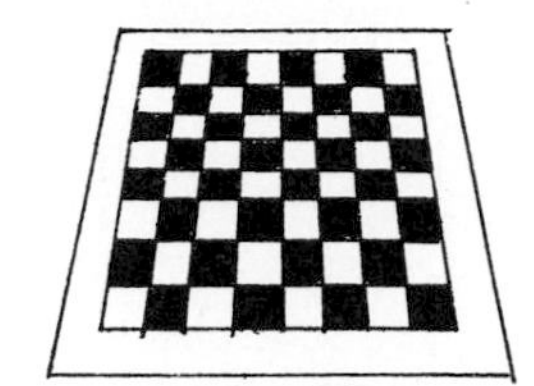

Almost at eye level with table.

Circles also change shape with your viewpoint.

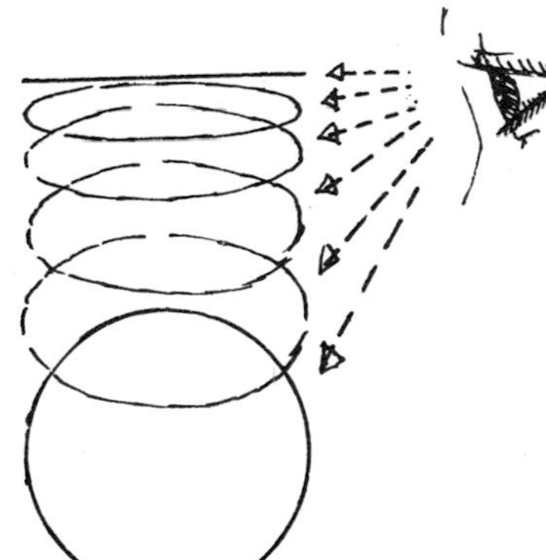

This is called an ellipse.

Just try to draw what you see!

Can you draw boxes on a tiled floor? Make the vanishing point at the top of your page.

3D EFFECT

One way of showing that an object is solid (three-dimensional), is by adding contours or wraparound lines. They show thickness and make things look real.

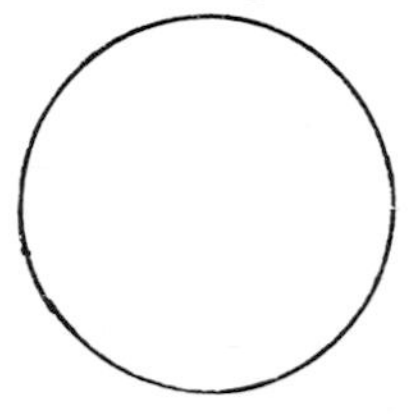

An empty circle...

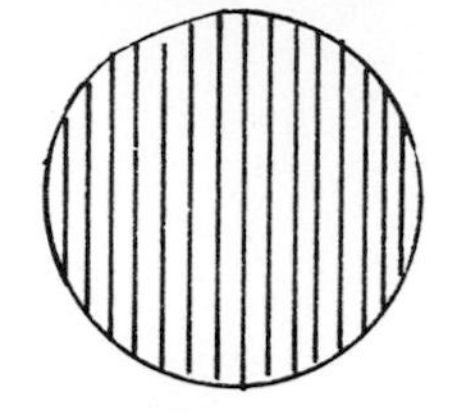

more interesting, but flat

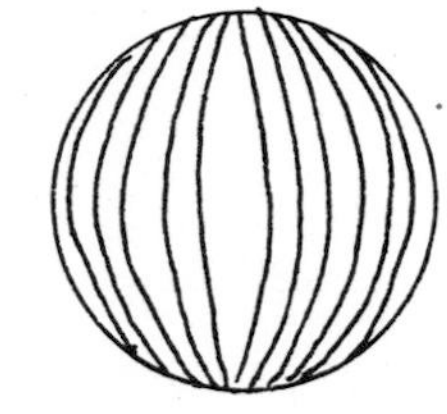

now it looks solid (3D).

A few lines may be enough...

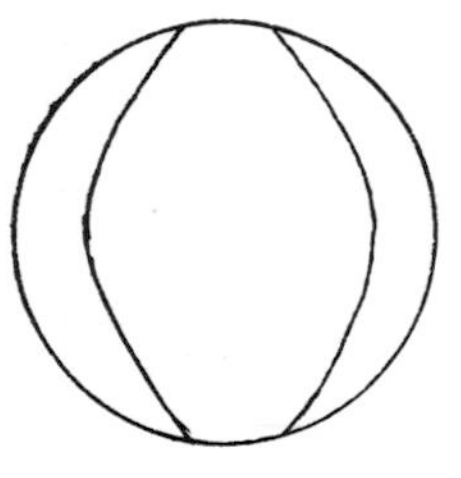

for a lovely ball...

for lots of body...

for a lifebelt.

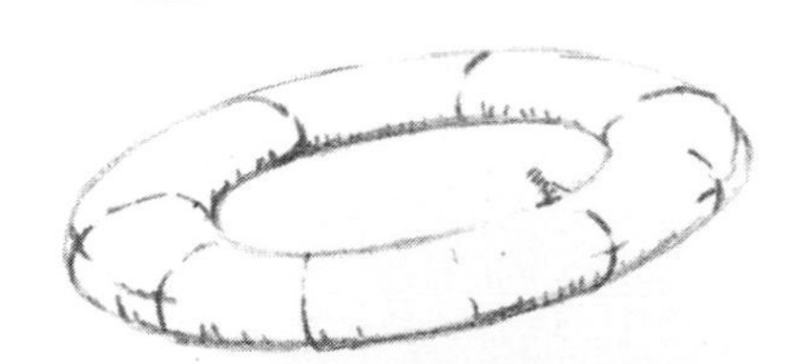

Using wraparound lines, draw a man holding a balloon. Make the balloon look exciting by drawing many lines around it.

Contour lines can make objects appear to be shaped in many ways — bent, curved, sunken, etc.

MATERIALS AND STYLE

Really, you only need anything that can make marks and a relatively blank piece of paper. Experiment!

Holding your drawing tool in different ways can help you develop many different styles.

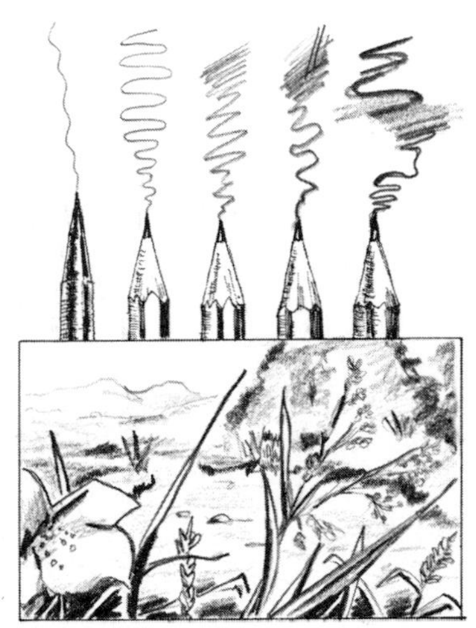

pencil

felt tip pen

charcoal

ink

Use many different types of paper to see what effects and textures you can find.

DETAIL

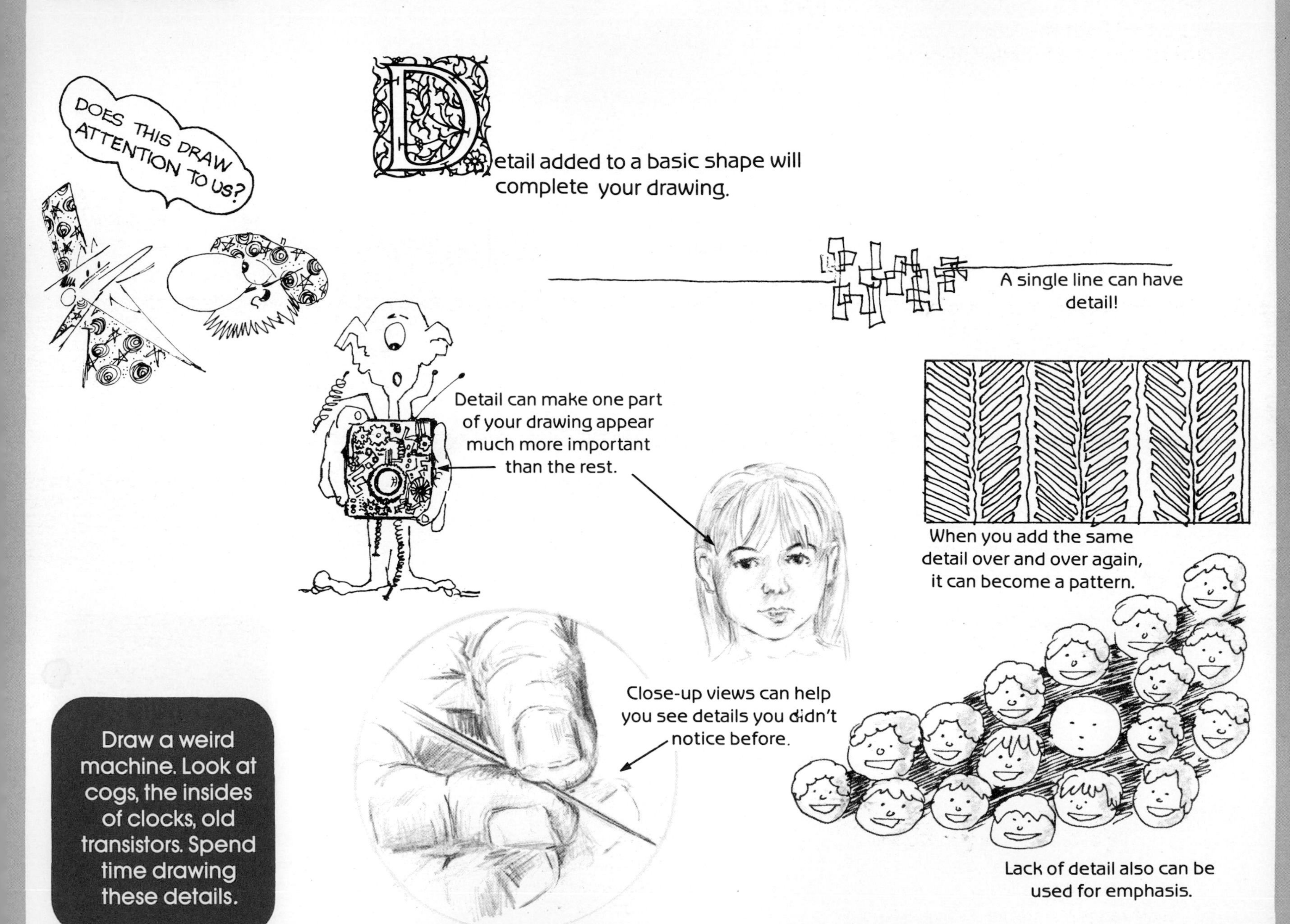

Detail added to a basic shape will complete your drawing.

A single line can have detail!

Detail can make one part of your drawing appear much more important than the rest.

When you add the same detail over and over again, it can become a pattern.

Close-up views can help you see details you didn't notice before.

Lack of detail also can be used for emphasis.

Draw a weird machine. Look at cogs, the insides of clocks, old transistors. Spend time drawing these details.

EMPHASIS

There's often one part of your drawing more important than the rest. Here are some different ways of emphasising that important part.

See the effect of a little black against white, or a little white against black.

There's less emphasis when there's a balance of white and black.

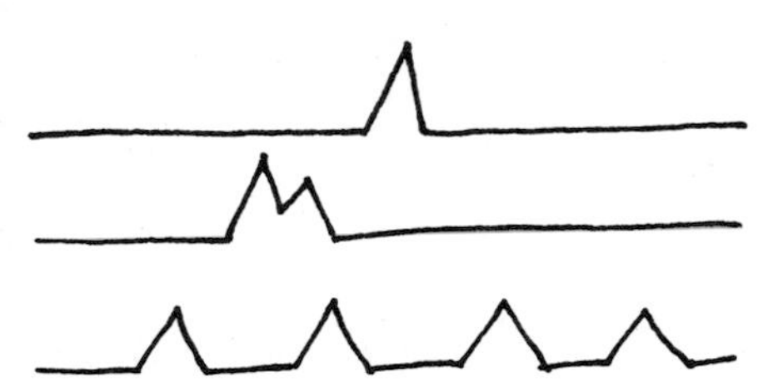

One bump creates emphasis. More destroys it!

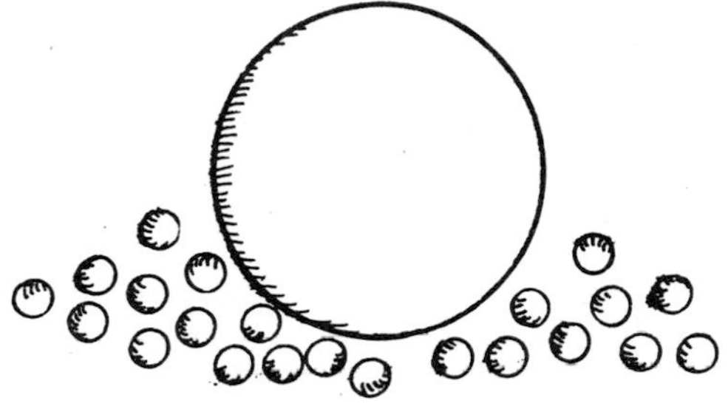

Something of an obviously different size draws attention to itself.

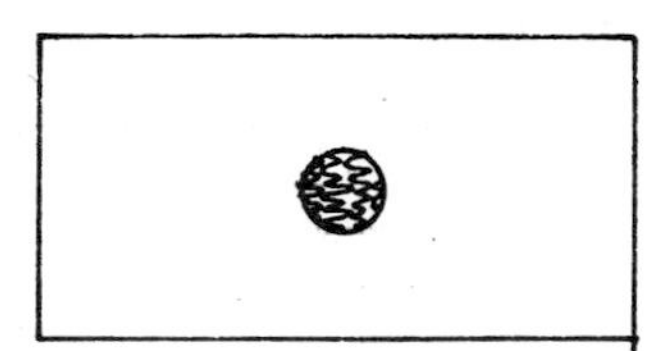

Detail or lack of detail can also make a strong point.

Deliberate distortion certainly causes us to look again.

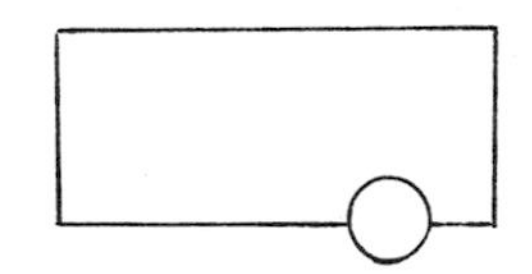

Which side is emphasised here?

Don't forget that your background can also be emphasised.

Draw a picture of your family, giving more attention to one person. How — size, distortion or detail?

MEASURING AND OBSERVING

To draw well, you need to look carefully at your subject and keep its proportions the same.

Draw from life wherever possible. Practise by drawing common objects.

Look for shadows on and under objects — even your half-eaten apple!

Notice where light comes from

To help you draw what you see, prop up your drawing. Look much more at the subject than at your drawing.

By standing in front of your house and using pencil measurements, draw an accurate, detailed study. Don't forget to use light and shadow.

Use your pencil to measure, compare and judge proportions.

1. Hold it straight out in front of you with a stiff arm, and close one eye.

2. By sliding your thumb along it you can compare measurements (e.g. height to width).

Keeping a sketchbook helps to record what you see.

3. Check proportions on your page.

COMPOSITION

Plan your drawing by selecting an arrangement or a point of view that makes the picture look interesting and keeps the viewer's attention within the frame.

The size and direction of your paper are your first composition problems.

With a model or a still life, arrange the subjects and then draw.

Experiment with composition. Where does the centre of interest fall?

Static – drawing is too centred.

Dynamic – altering the interest centre has made the picture more interesting.

In building your pictures, get involved. Have subjects close, and show movement. Size and overlapping are important.

A view frame may help you find the scene that looks best.

Use your hands if you wish.

Compose a picture showing an outside game. Try a dynamic composition that shows movement and has at least one figure close to the viewer.

TECHNIQUES

Start drawing with light pencil pressure (so you can just see it). First work out where things will go. Then build your drawing up gradually, concentrating on the whole page.

Don't correct mistakes immediately. Wait until you have the right line before erasing. Use a soft rubber for pencil or charcoal.

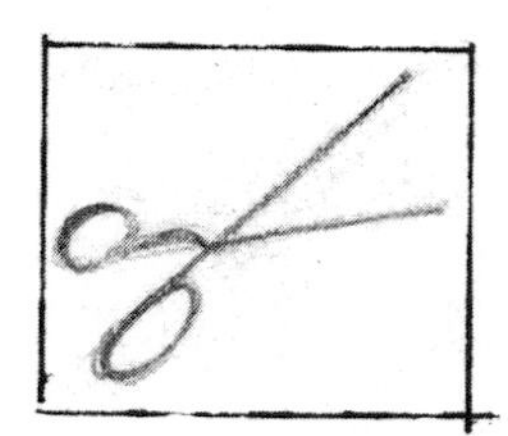

Plan your composition.

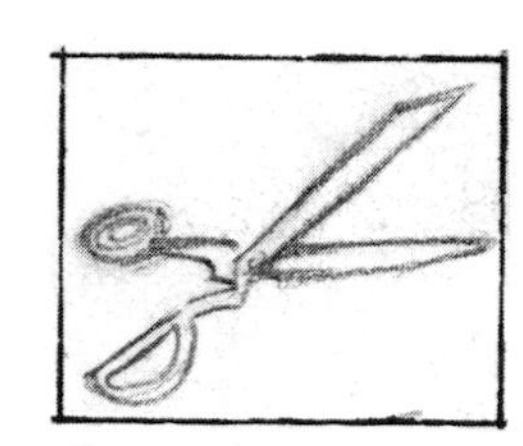

In light pencil, develop shape, contour and shadows.

Add detail, then erase unwanted pencil lines.

Experiment with different styles.

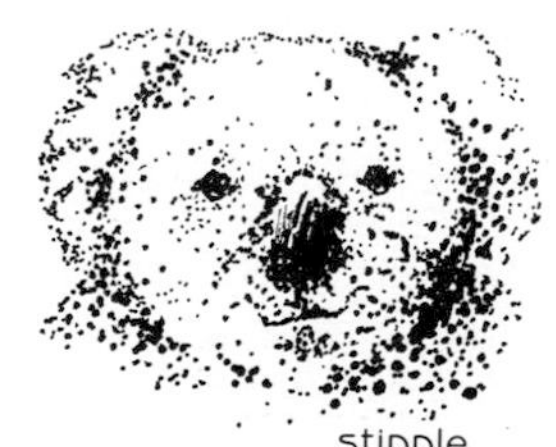

stipple

side pencil

directional lines

cross-hatching

hatching

curved lines

Draw a picture of your pet lightly in pencil. Decide on a style. Now complete the picture, background and shadows included, using only that style throughout.

FIGURES — INTRODUCTION

Drawing the figure needs close observation and careful measurement — and let's not forget practice!

Posing — Proportions — Measuring

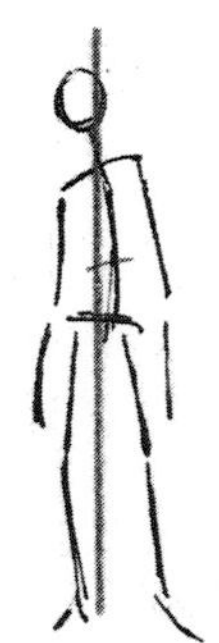

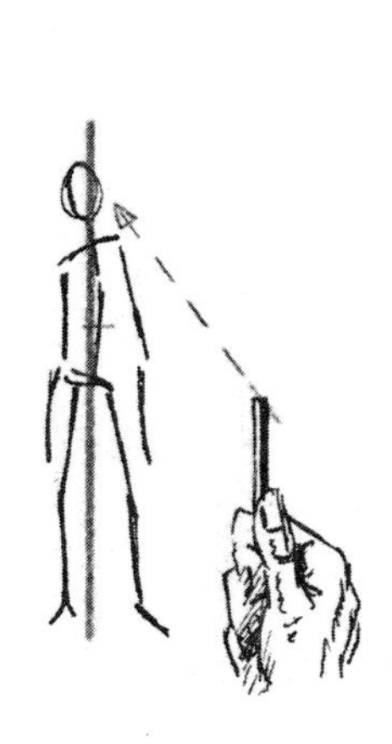

1. Draw a vertical line. Observe pose (how the figure is arranged) in relation to this line.

2. Draw the pose. Keep lines light and quick.

3. Check proportions, using your pencil to measure.

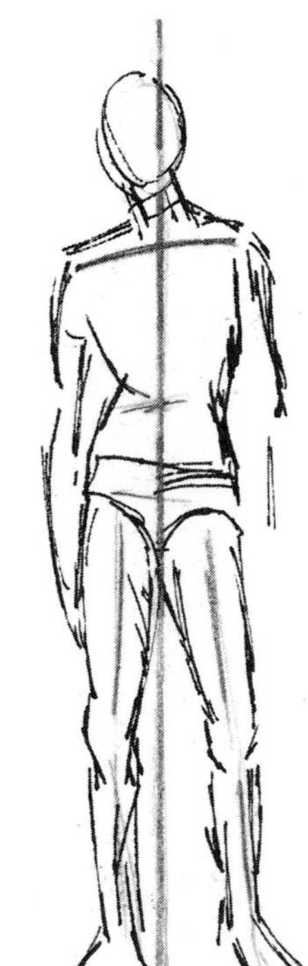

4. Draw many lines to discover the right place. You can always erase later — and perhaps many lines will look better anyway.

Always try to draw from life. Either have someone model, or sketch actions quickly.

A sketchbook is handy.

Make it real. Draw each part of the figure with the same emphasis throughout. Always concentrate on the whole rather than its parts. Avoid detail until completion.

Draw a friend. Every line you make must be drawn over 5 times in the same direction. Notice how your style changes.

FIGURES – PROPORTIONS

Proportions in the figure are found by comparison. The accepted unit of measurement is the head. For individual subjects, use your pencil to measure the head and make comparisons within the figure according to this. Here is a guide.

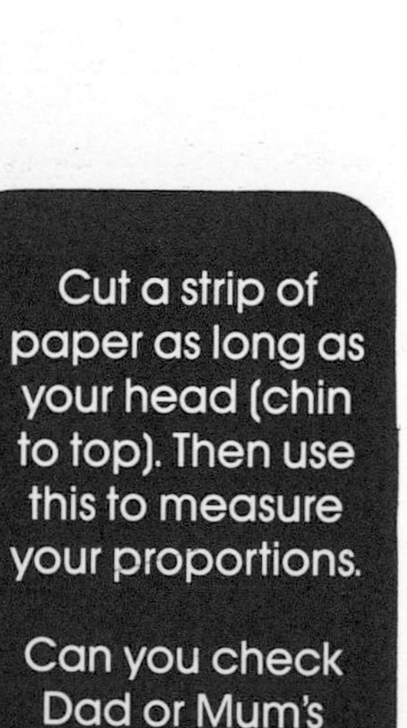

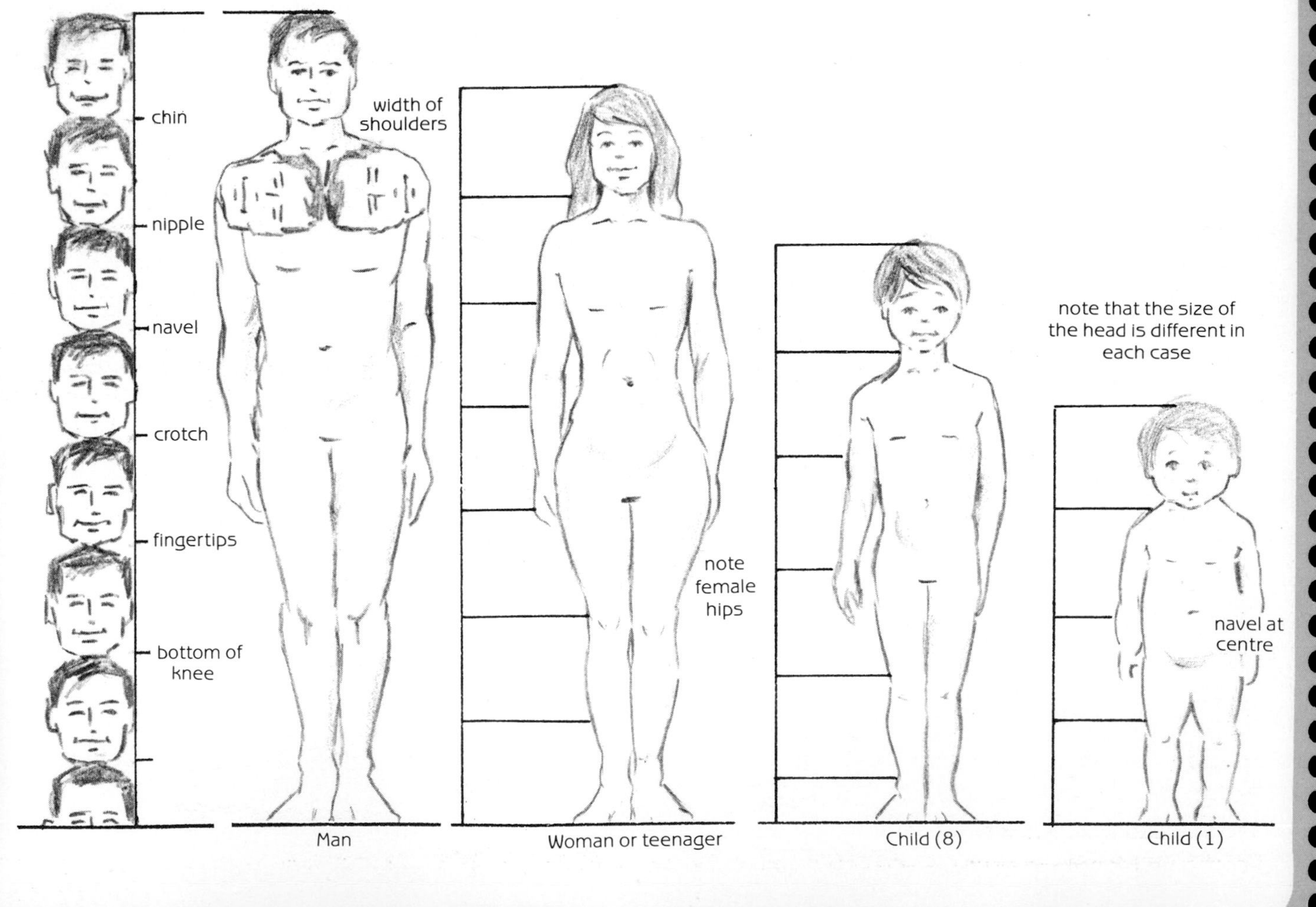

FIGURES – STARTING POINTS

Look carefully at the pose. Determine the main lines, and then start with those. Always draw the whole figure. There are many different ways to begin. Find one that suits you.

Notice the knees!

Sideways, a stick figure can look like this.

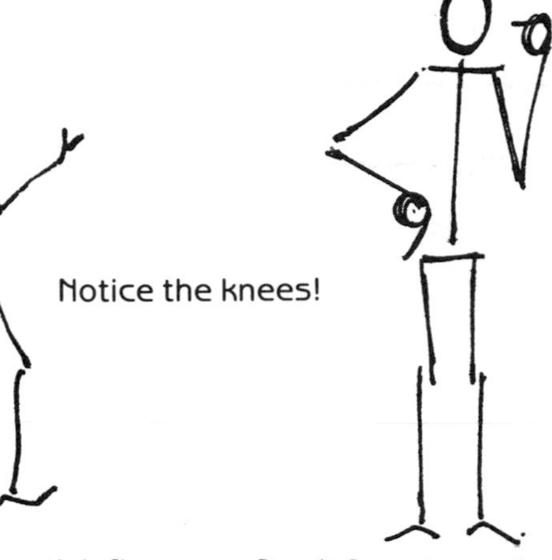

Don't forget my shoulders and hips!

I was drawn without looking at the page. I may look funny, but it's good practice drawing what you see.

Draw contour lines around the figure.

What about using shapes?

Can you add to your stick figure?

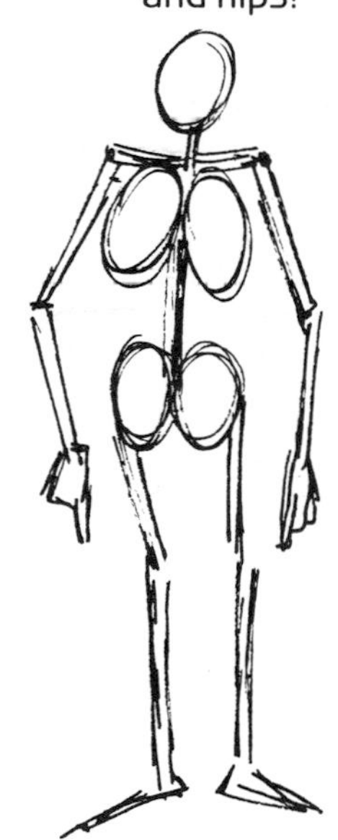

Double it up!

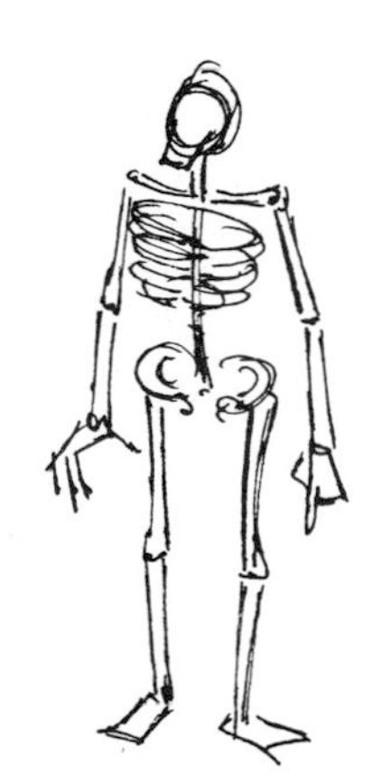

Skeleton figure.

Using a viewing frame, fill in the space around the figure. Add detail later.

Have a friend model 4 different poses for you. Take no more than 2 minutes for each pose. Now try to pose your model according to your drawings. You shouldn't have to break bones!

HEADS

One way to learn about heads is to measure and observe your own. Use a mirror.

1. Draw an oval. Use a central axis line, as you did for the figure. Draw a line cutting this at right angles, halfway down.

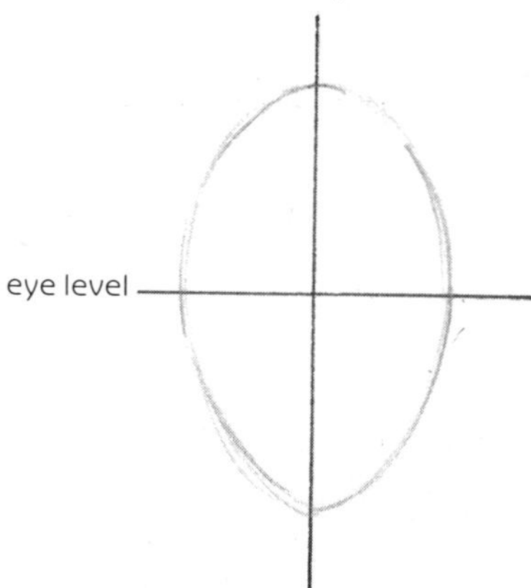

2. Use your own head to examine different measurements.

Thickness of hair may vary.

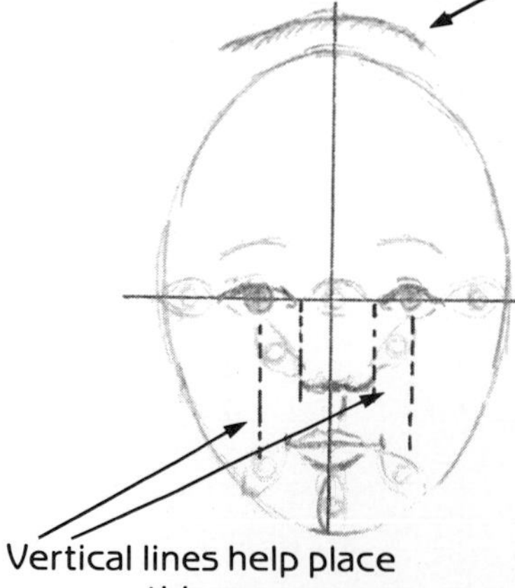

Use the eye to compare and measure distances.

Vertical lines help place things.

Draw a portrait of a model looking up. This will test your skills of observation. You'll also see the neck clearly.

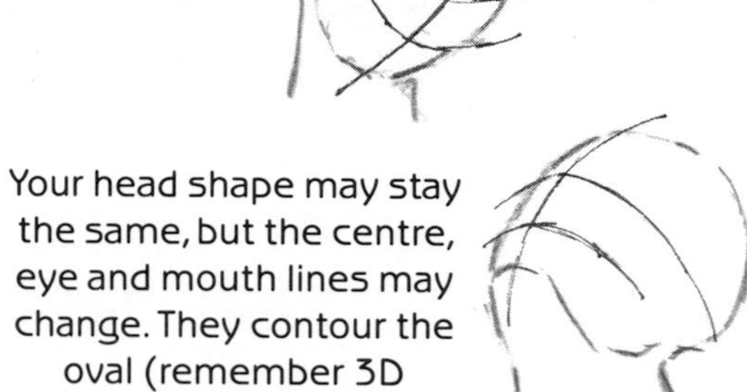

Your head shape may stay the same, but the centre, eye and mouth lines may change. They contour the oval (remember 3D effect).

Chin may cover the neck in part.

The neck slopes into the shoulders.

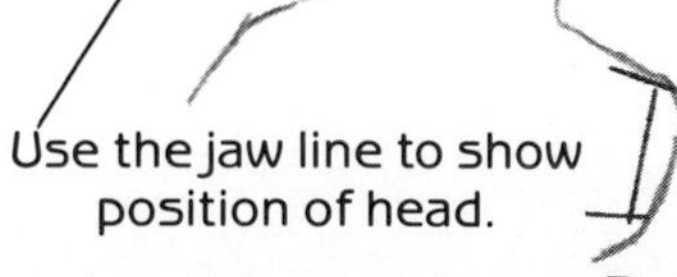

Use the jaw line to show position of head.

Remember the back — the part of the head we forget!

T-shape tells us which part is in front.

PROFILES

Sometimes it can be easier to capture a person's likeness by drawing the head from the side. The features can be seen in outline. Don't forget to draw the back of the head. Use your own head to check proportions.

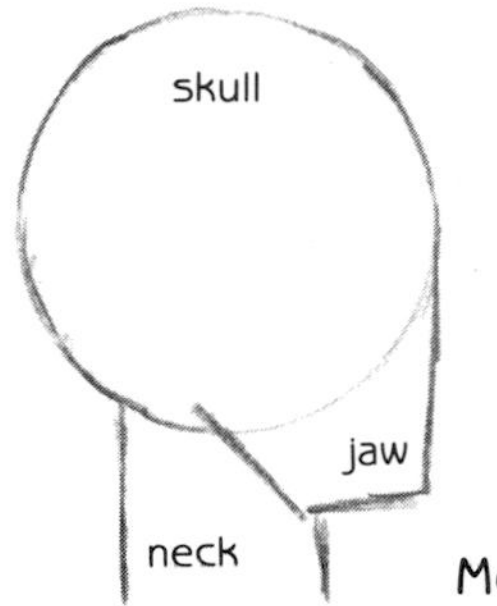

Measure level and distance with pencil.

Can you work out how this was done?

Notice where the eye sits in relation to ears and nose.

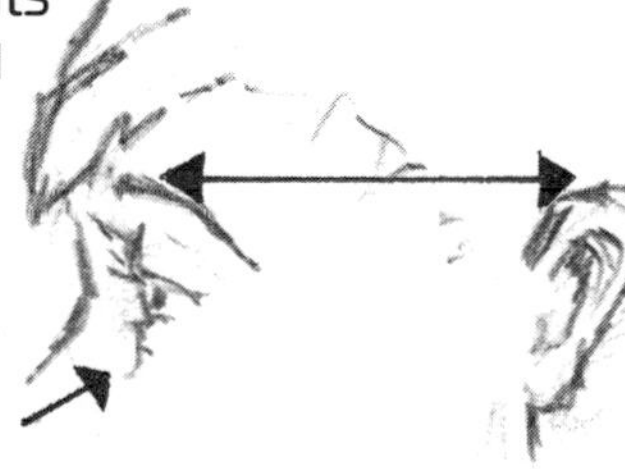

Note the shape of the nose and the space around it.

If in doubt about drawing a profile (or object) look at the space around it and draw the outline!

Draw another profile, facing this one. Can you do it exactly the same, but in reverse?

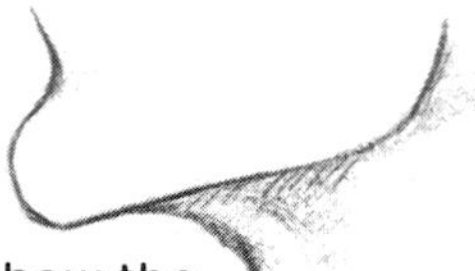

Look carefully at how the jaw and neck join.

Draw profiles of your family or friends. Then see whether they recognise each other.

FACES

At each step, work the face as a whole, with the same emphasis on each part. Keep your lines light.

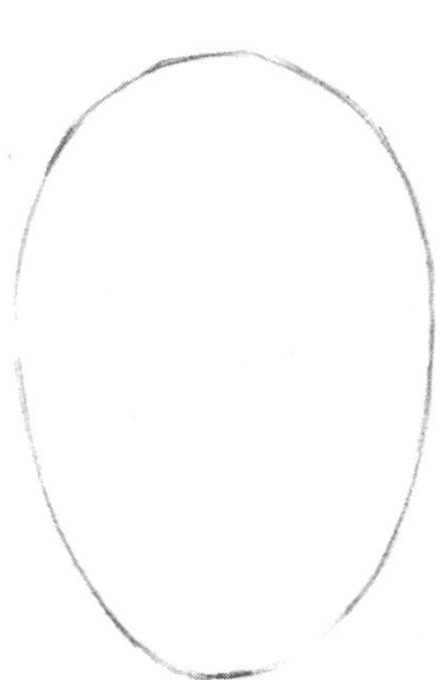
1. Draw an egg shape.

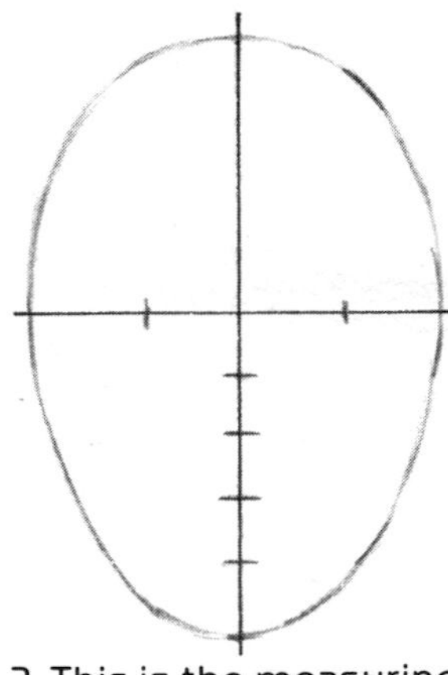
2. This is the measuring stage.

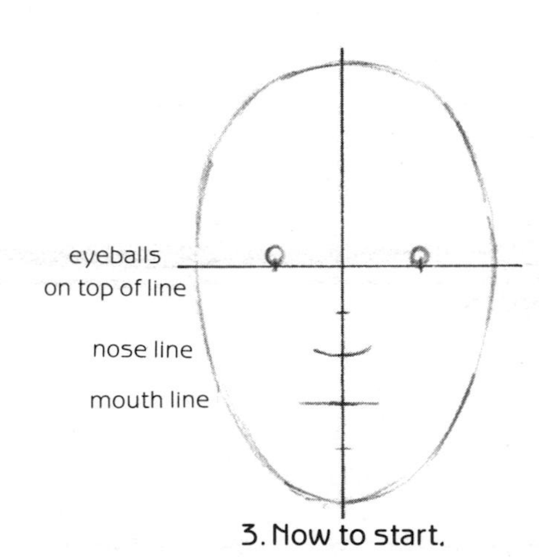

3. Now to start.

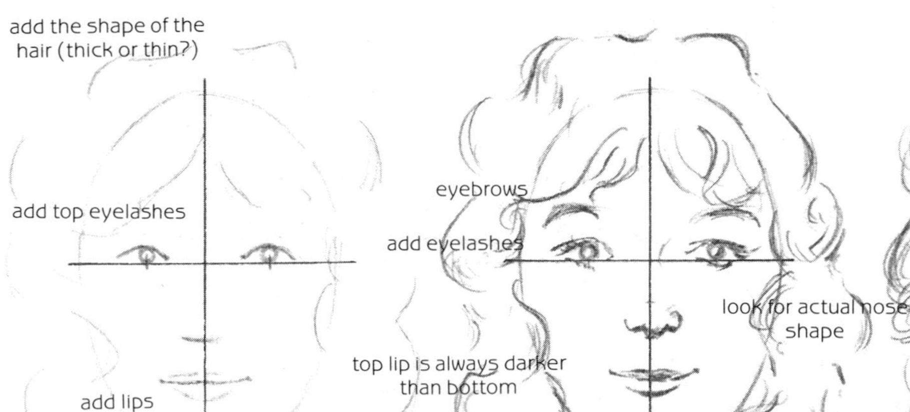

4. It's starting to take shape.

5. Adding details.

6. Finishing the face.

This is a good chance to use a model. (Remember, you can use a mirror.) Try out this method one step at a time.

PORTRAITS

Close observation and time will help you produce a likeness to the subject. You're telling a story, not just producing a photograph, remember.

The traditional three-quarter view.

1. Begin by roughing out the shape of the head and facial positions.

2. Begin working in main shapes and shadow.

3. Look for individual detail. Work lightly, building to solid line when likeness appears.

A light helps you draw shadows and makes your drawing look real.

Try a self portrait. Set up a mirror so that you can see yourself without moving. Take your time and draw.

EYES, MOUTH AND NOSE

A step-by-step approach to drawing features.

I THINK YOU HAVE TO PUT THEM ON THE SAME PAGE.

Draw the eyes carefully. Look closely as you build each detail.

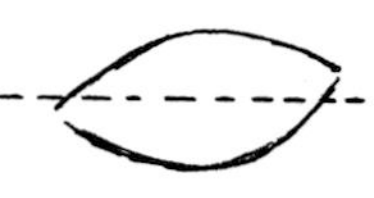

draw a football, point it

check the actual shape

add lashes

put in the iris and pupil

shade the iris

add eyelids and other details

Work out the angles from the outside edge of the eyes to the tip of nose (use your pencil). Does it look right?

draw a line to show the width of the bottom of the nose

get the shape right here

add nostrils

shade to show the ball of the nose

add lines pointing down to the edge of the lips

shade beneath to show how the nose sticks out

Look for the distance from nose to upper lip. Check the length of the mouth.

length of the mouth

get the line and distance between lips right

add shape of top lip

add shape of bottom lip

add corners and other details and shade under the bottom lip to show depth

Using a mirror, build a step-by-step picture of your eyes only, as large as you can.

NOSE AND HAIR

Two features that may spoil your drawing are the nose and the hair. Done well, they can make your face very realistic and lifelike.

These noses are fine for cartoons only.

Shadows make noses appear solid.

Pay attention to the shape.

Use your pencil to judge the position of the tip of the nose.

Draw the shape of the hair as a flat mass. Detail strands later.

Take your time. Draw strands of hair. Concentrate on the style

Hair has thickness.

Use lines to show light hair.

Use blocks of pencil/ink to show dark hair.

Turn your paper so that you draw sweeping lines from an inside curve. It gives a much freer line.

Using the tracing technique, draw the same face 5 times. Give your subject a new hairstyle each time. Copy styles from life or photographs if you wish.

EXPRESSIONS

The facial muscles react to happenings and are capable of showing many changes of mood in a short time. In drawing we try to capture these. Here are just some that are instantly recognised. Experiment to find more.

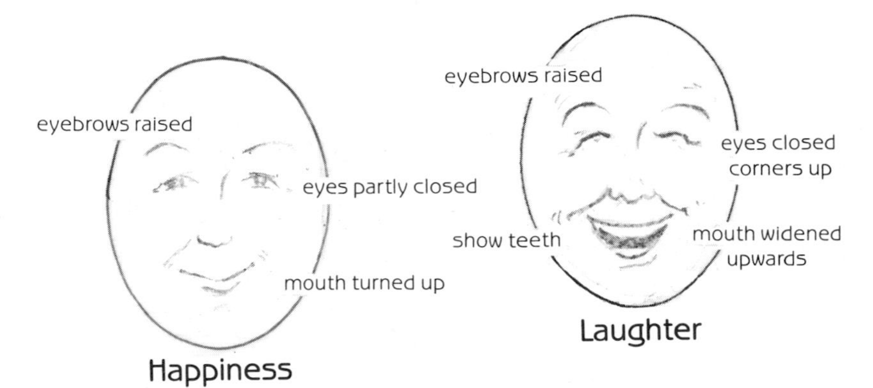

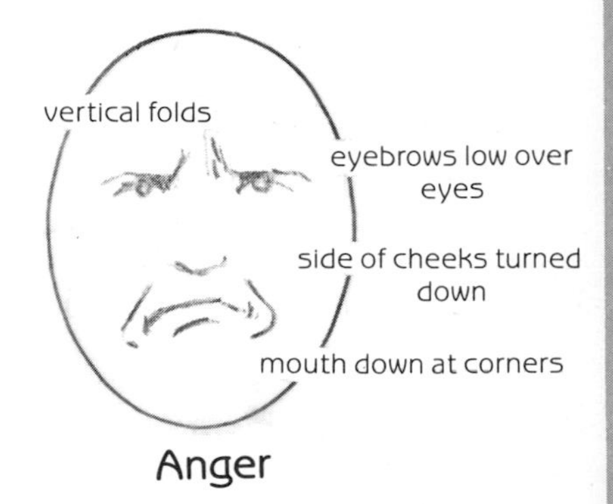

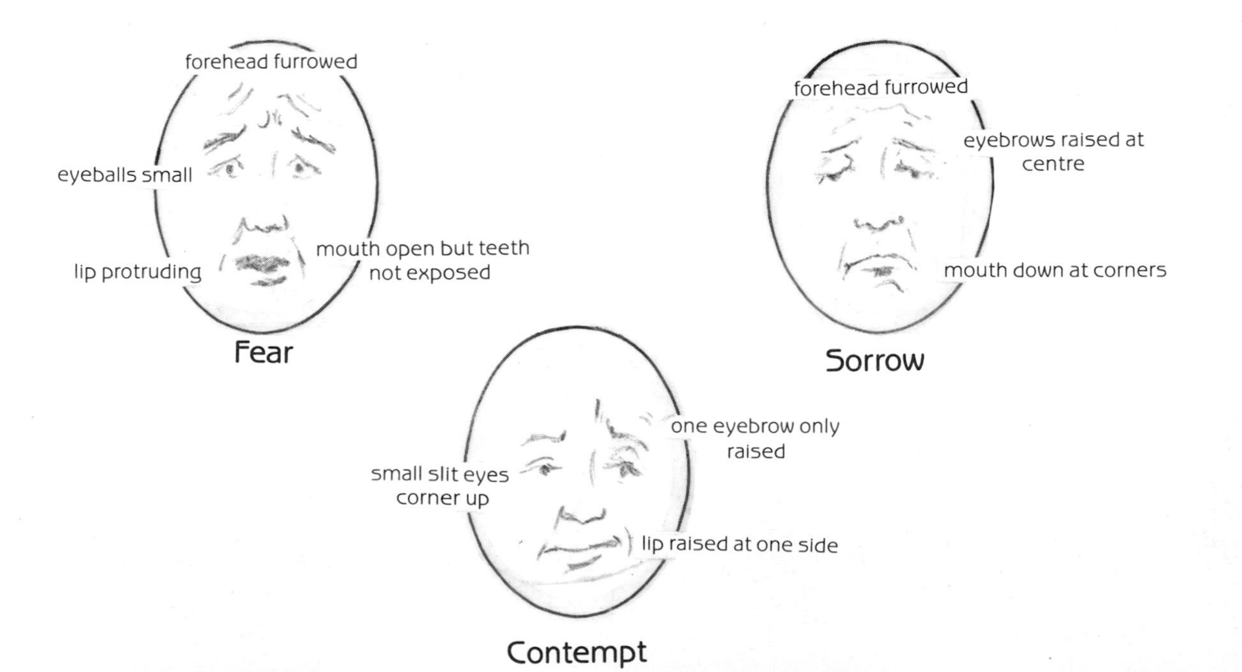

Using a mirror, draw yourself being angry or sad. You may like to complete the picture by showing the reasons.

DIFFERENT AGES

We show the age of a person through the face in many ways. The more you look, the more hints you'll find. Here are some things to look for.

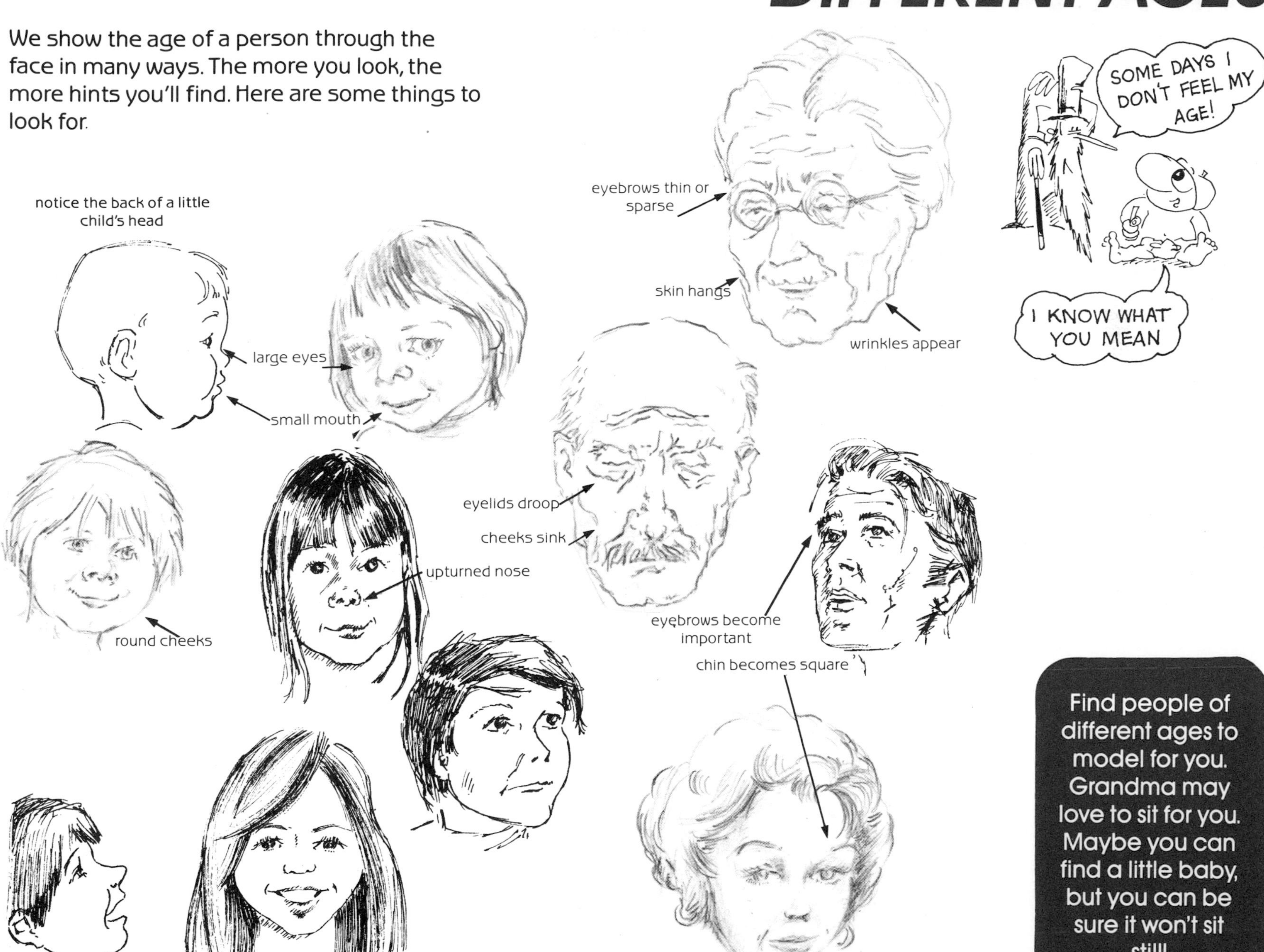

Find people of different ages to model for you. Grandma may love to sit for you. Maybe you can find a little baby, but you can be sure it won't sit still!

THE HANDS

You can always draw your own hand in any position you like!

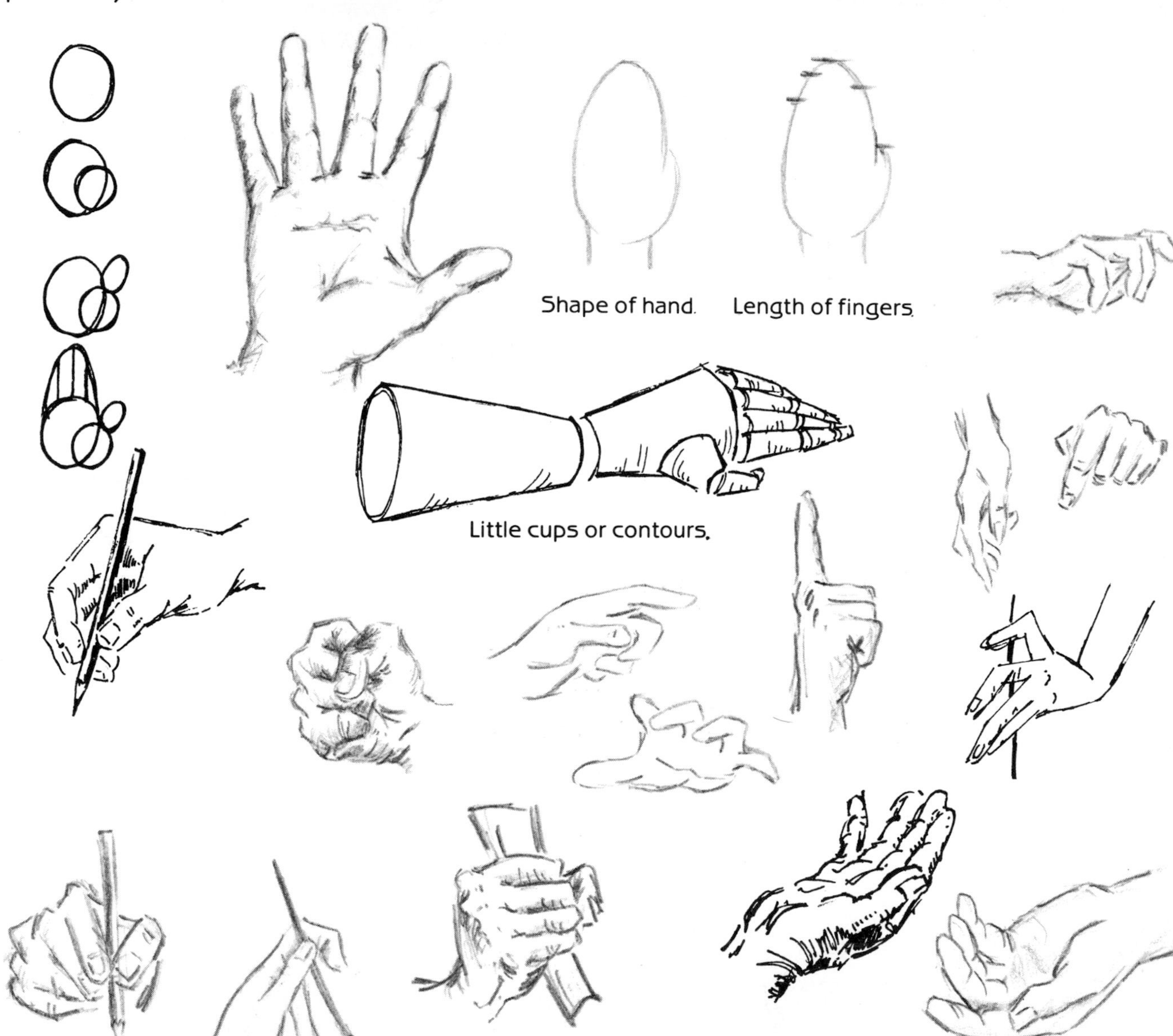

You become the model. Draw your own hand holding the drawing paper. Get the shape right — then add all the fine detail.

FEET AND SHOES

They give movement and balance to your figure, so take it one step at a time.

And there's nothing like drawing your own feet. Observe, observe, observe!

ARMS

WELL IT'S PRETTY 'ARMLESS!

Study arms carefully. Get the proportions right.

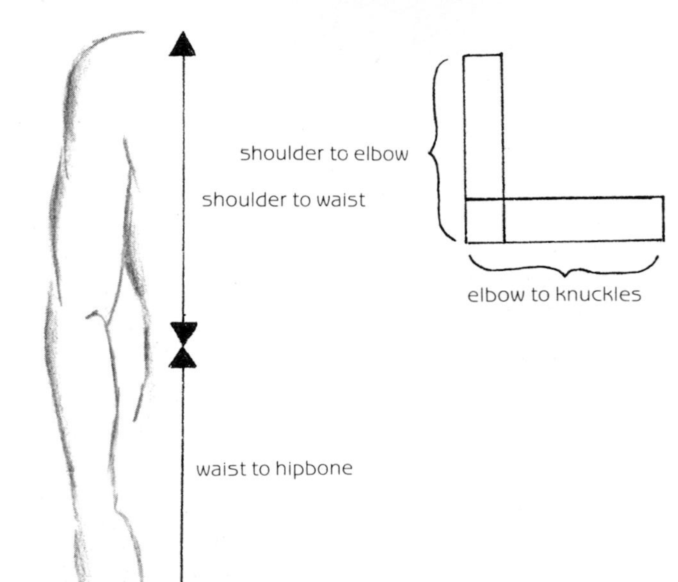

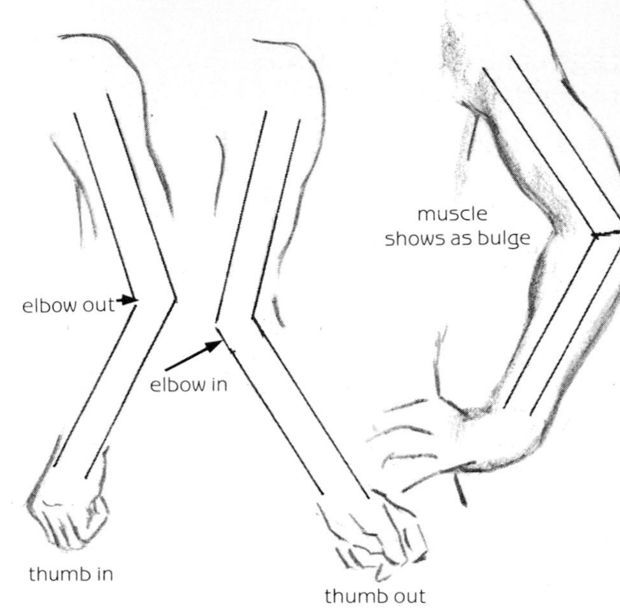

Can you draw yourself touching your toes? Where does your head come to?

What's wrong here?

Children's arms and legs (when compared with head size) are shorter than adults'.

LEGS

Legs are the longest limbs in the body – make them so!

Ways to start

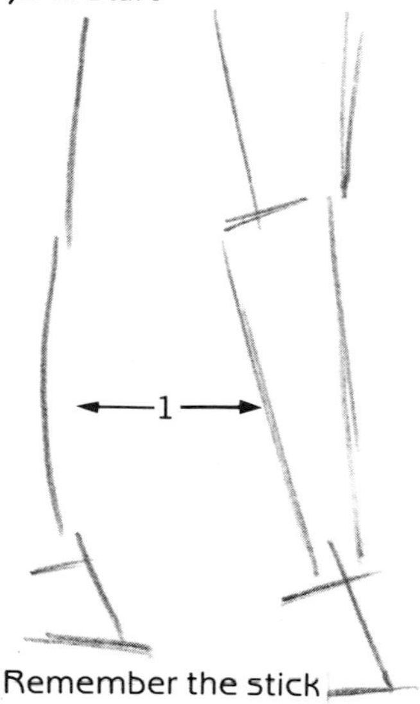

muscle

1

2

3

Remember the stick

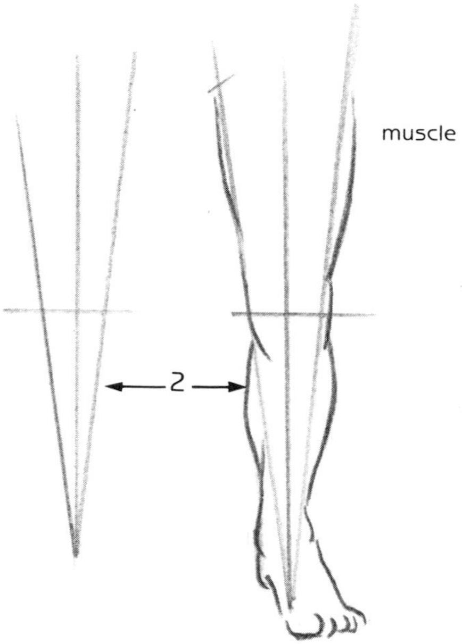

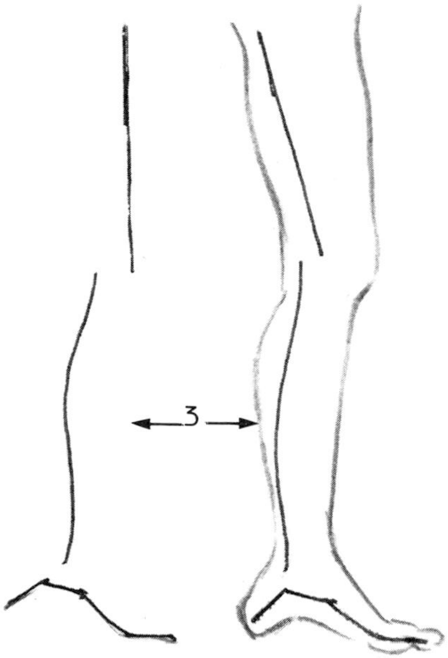

Side on

NOW THAT'S A BIG TRICK!

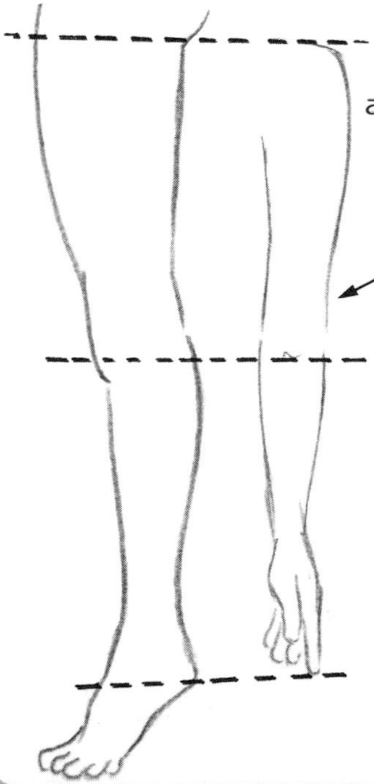

The length of a leg (to ankle) is the same as the length of an arm (to fingertips).

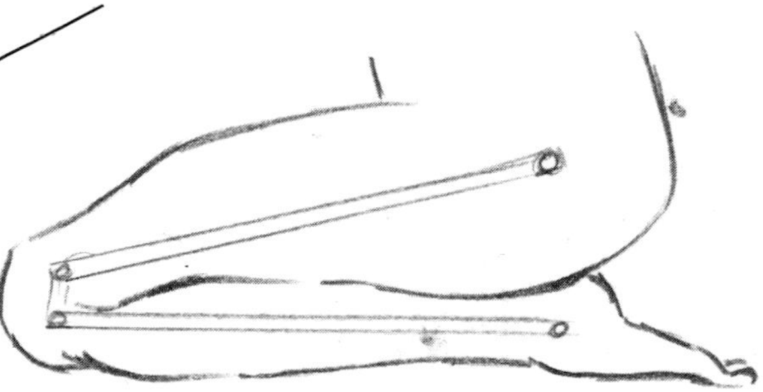

Notice overlapping lines.

Lie down on a large sheet of paper (e.g. newspaper) and have someone trace around you. Now you'll see the size of your legs.

BUILDING THE FIGURE

Try to draw each part of the figure with the same emphasis, always concentrating on the whole rather than the parts. Avoid detail until the last step. Give parts the same amount of detail, unless you wish to emphasise an area.

1. Draw pose

2. Add contours

3. Choose style

4. Add detail

Build your figure on a very large sheet of paper. Pay attention to the steps, and build it carefully.

POSITIONS

The good thing about using a model is that you can arrange the pose to suit your drawing.

Don't forget the back view!

Have your model pose, then you move to the best viewpoint.

Use objects such as chairs, rugs. These become part of your drawing.

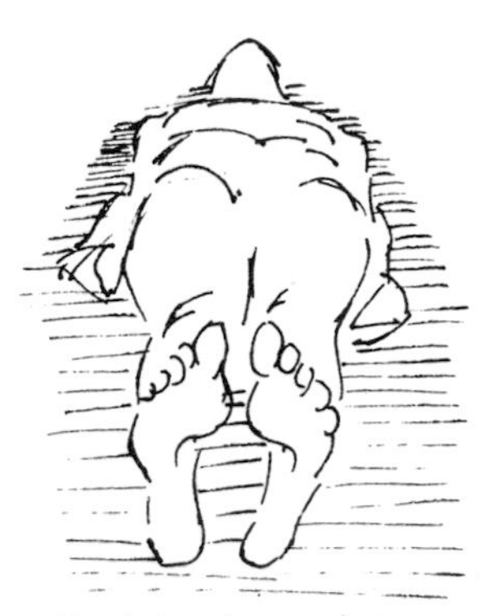

Certain viewpoints require us to distort proportions to show the pose correctly. This is called foreshortening.

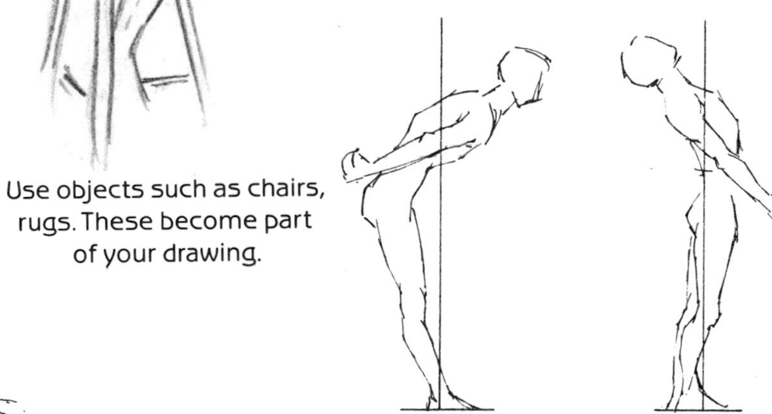

Use centre axis to show weight.

Make careful note of light and shadows.

Keep the surrounding area free of distractions.

Try a reclining figure.

If you can't get models to 'sit' for you, look through magazines. Build up a scrapbook of different positions – sitting, standing, reclining, etc.

SITUATIONS

To draw a person moving is very difficult (they can't stand still for you). Look for the main line that tells the pose. Sketch rapidly.

Check the balance of your figure by trying the pose yourself. If you fall over, correct your drawing.

You can find many good situations to draw by looking at magazines and family photos. Copy one you really like!

GROUPS

Most pictures need more than one person to tell the story. These ideas may help you save time.

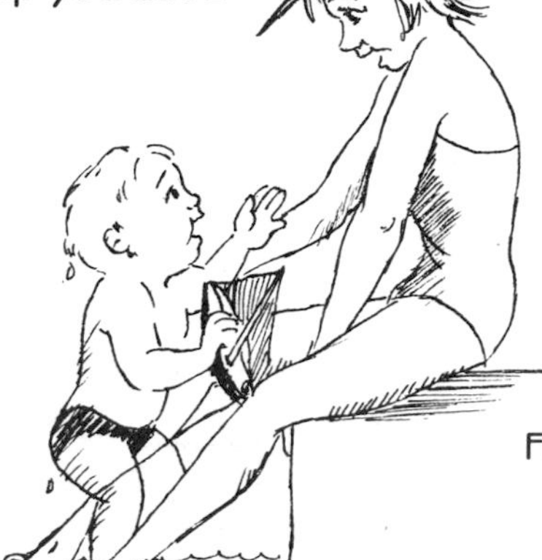

Eye contact helps to tell the story of a small group.

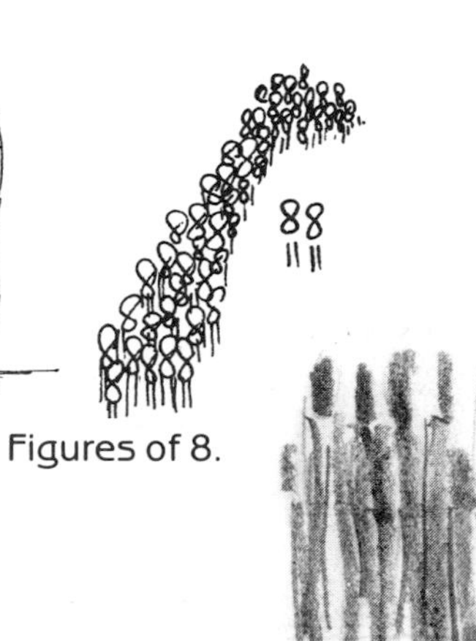

Figures of 8.

Shading.

Paper textures can help you to draw large-crowd shapes.

The amount of detail you use is up to you and the time you wish to spend.

Boxes.

A moving crowd using X's and O's.

Lines.

If you want a big group, try drawing a group of spectators or a football team. A small group could be just two friends.

CLOTHING

Clothes give the figure shape and tell much about the subject. Pay close attention to detail.

Folds are important.

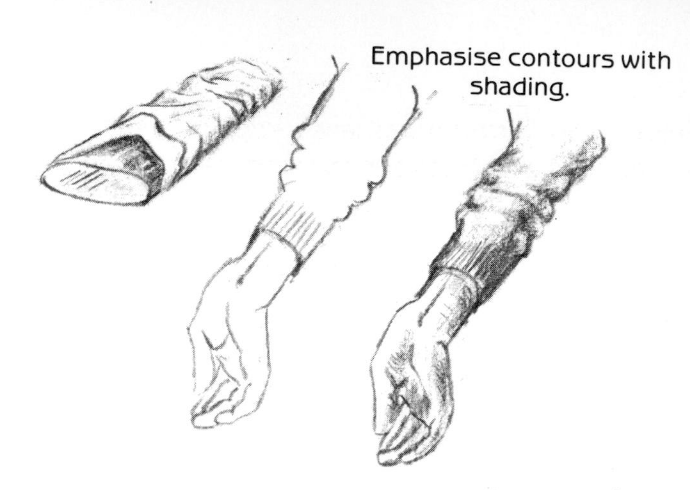

Emphasise contours with shading.

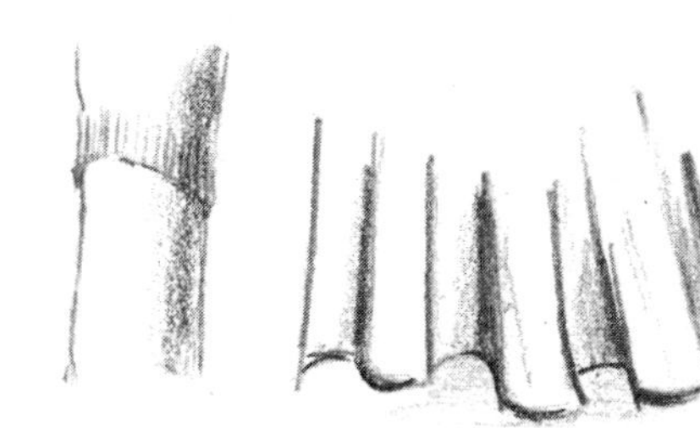

Draw ribbing and pleats

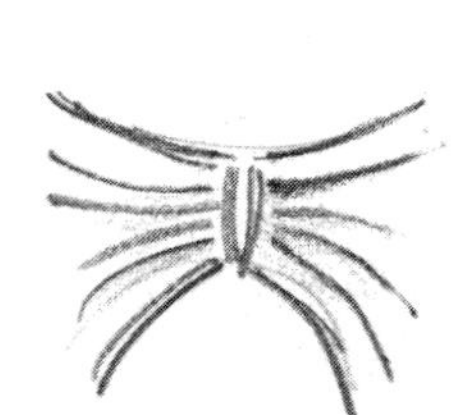

Look for creases and folds.

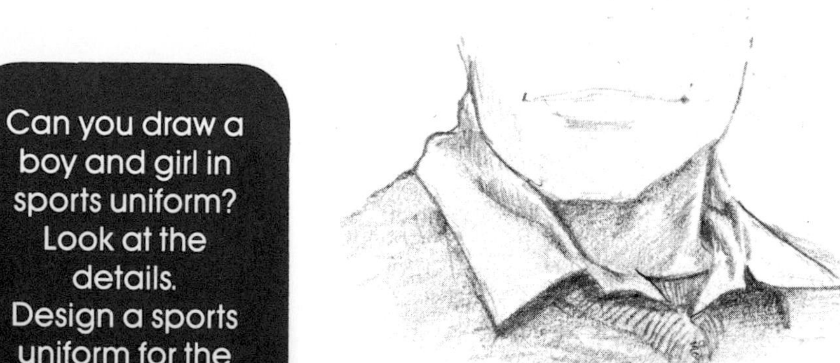

Notice shadow!

What a difference some detail makes to a T-shirt.

Can you draw a boy and girl in sports uniform? Look at the details. Design a sports uniform for the year 2000, maybe for a new sport!

STILL LIFE

Selecting and arranging the objects for a still life is a good way to experiment as well as observe.

Crumpled paper or material make interesting shapes to draw.

Think of a subject!

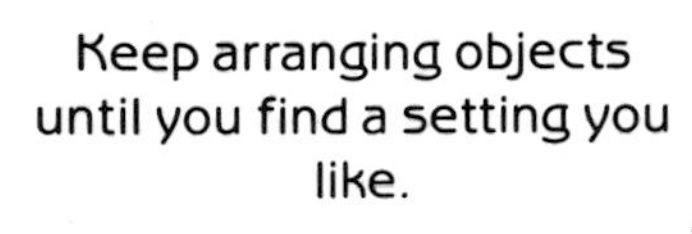

Keep arranging objects until you find a setting you like.

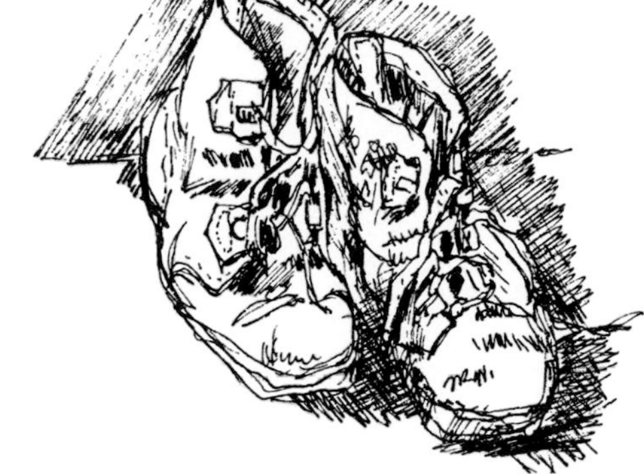

Old used things make good subjects.

WHAT BELONGS TO WHOM?

Notice overlapping.

Try drawing the space around objects.

Choose a very small object to draw, e.g. a key. By observing closely, draw it as large as your paper will allow.

ANIMALS

Take it one step at a time. Build up to your final drawing.

Draw a horse lightly in pencil – perhaps from the sports section of the newspaper. Now, put a rider on it.

MORE ANIMALS

Isn't it time your pet got into the picture? Make your animal famous – draw your own pet portrait!

BIRDS

Open your eyes! — Here is a subject you'll find everywhere...but you must be quiet!

Make your own bird book. Draw a page of different beaks or feet. Use books and observe birds closely.

TREES

We are surrounded by many different types of trees, wherever we live. Study them closely.

This is a start, not a finish.

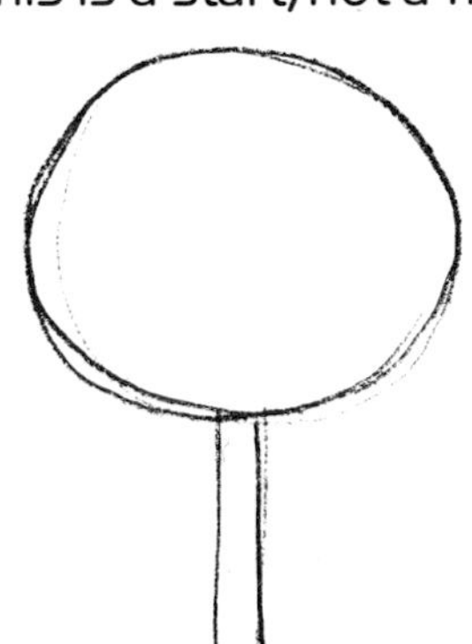

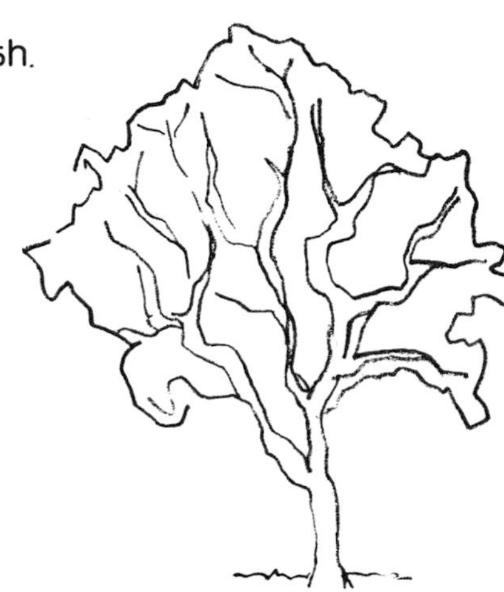

Side-on pencil to suggest tone and mass.

Lines for trunks.

Shading for branches.

Trees in the distance.

There is nothing like a tree to test your drawing skills. Draw a collection of different trees to use in your next landscape.

PLANTS

They're found inside as well as outside, they flower, they bear fruit and they're beaut to draw!

The same leaf seen at different angles and stages.

Ways to draw clumps of grass.

A flower looks different when drawn from different angles.

Study an indoor plant closely. Draw it in detail, adding only what background is needed to make it stand out.

Ferns begin with skeleton lines.

Different styles of drawing can give different feelings.

FLOWERS

Use your eyes when studying particular flowers – you'll find no two exactly the same.

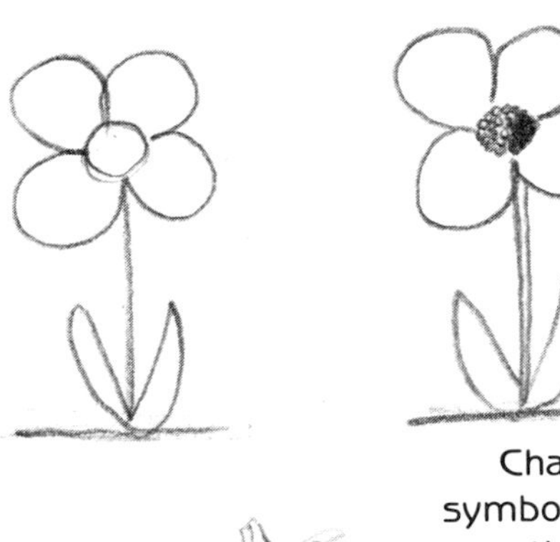

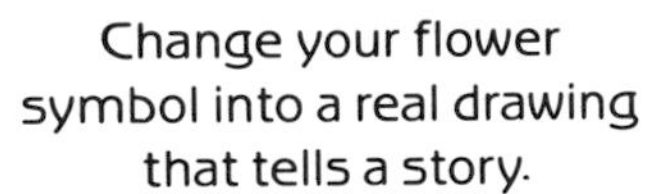

Change your flower symbol into a real drawing that tells a story.

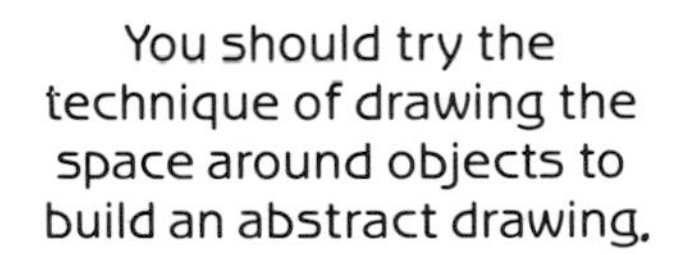

You should try the technique of drawing the space around objects to build an abstract drawing.

Many famous artists have painted flowers. See how many different styles you can find.

LANDSCAPES

Let's work outside — you probably need the fresh air by now anyway!

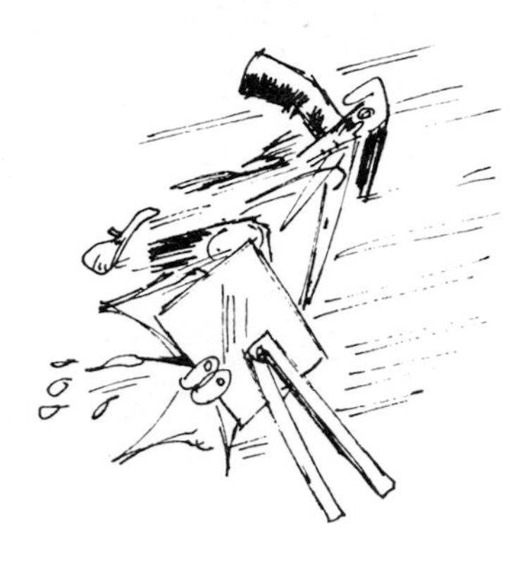

Same scene — more interest.

A 'side-pencil' sky.

Ocean built of waves drawn with the side of the pencil.

Dark is closer.

Cross-hatching shows the planes of rocks.

Experiment with different paper and different materials.

Side-pencil wire line added.

BUILDINGS

Your town is full of good models. Buildings do not move and are made up of basic shapes.

Begin with your own house. It's convenient!

Try a construction site — there are lines everywhere.

I SEE YOU'RE BUILDING A DRAWING AGAIN!

How about something old and broken down? Tell a story.

Don't forget to measure.

Use perspective.

Try a close-up study.

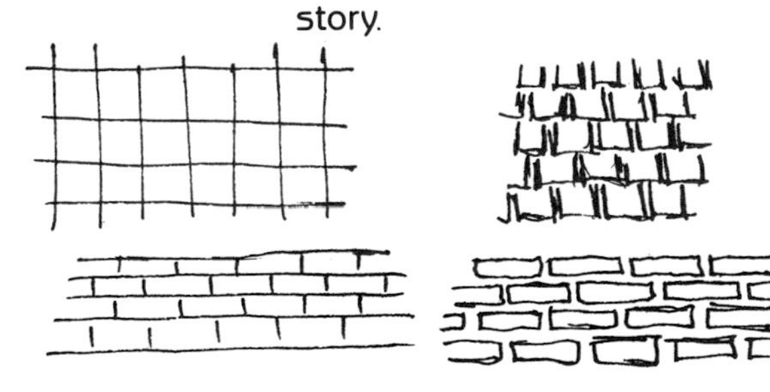

Begin with the basic shape, then spend time to add detail.

Study how things join up.

Look for reflections in glass.

Begin by copying an older-style house lightly. Now, using light and dark tones, change it into a haunted mansion!

CARS

How you draw gives your car a different character.

broken lines

scribbly, free lines

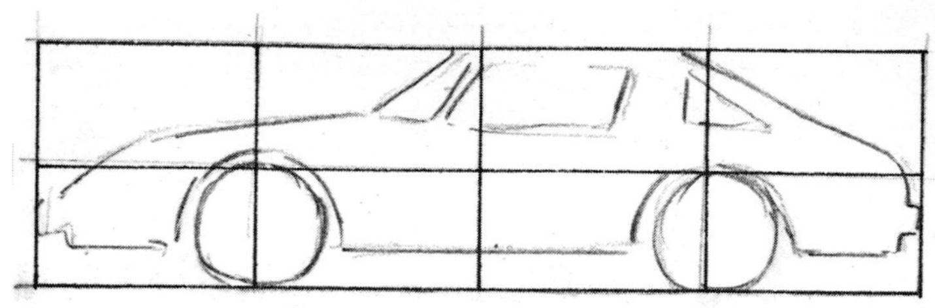
Using a grid to draw a car.

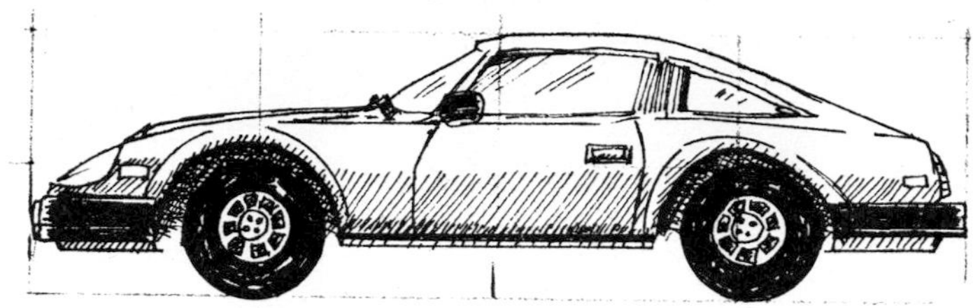

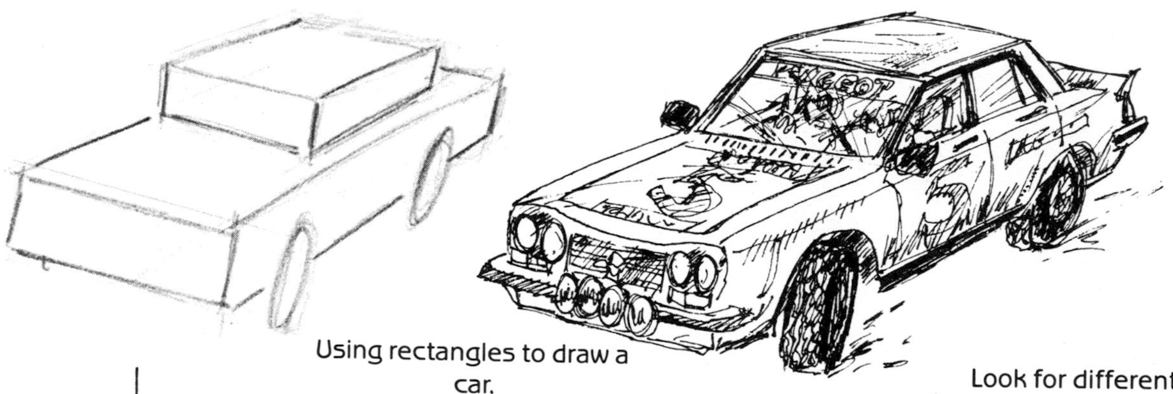
Using rectangles to draw a car.

Look for different angles.

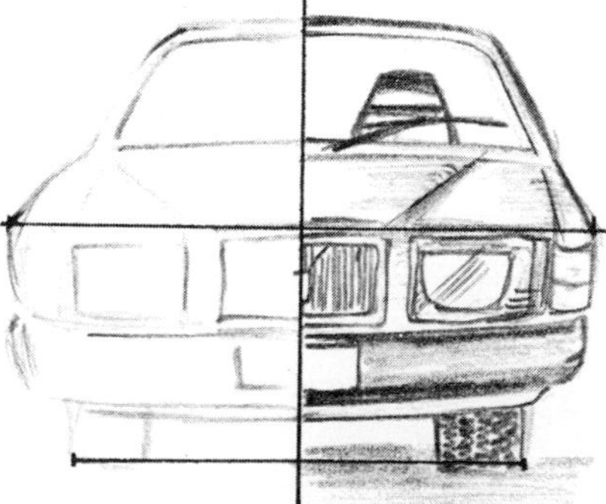
Try front-on drawing.

You need your best observation skills to keep up with all the new styles of cars.

You know the basic shapes for cars – now try designing your own.

VEHICLES

It's just a matter of drawing rectangles and boxes, then adding detail. Try drawing your straight lines without a ruler.

Scribble style

Remember perspective.

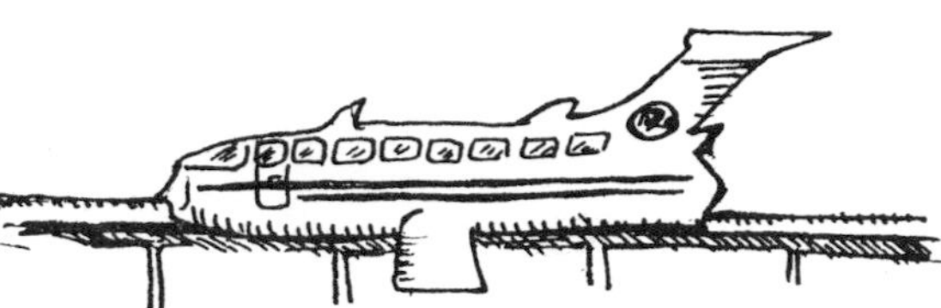

Try different angles.

Collect pictures from magazines and advertisements. Practise drawing these and adding your own detail.

BIKES AND BOATS

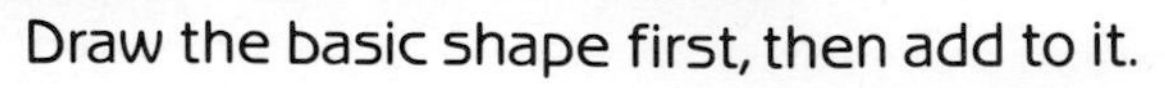

Draw the basic shape first, then add to it.

A very simple way to start. Two big circles and a frame (check your frame).

Off-centre shows action.

Your bike makes a great model – start as shown here, but make your drawing special!

The figure 8 shape can be a good way to start any boat.

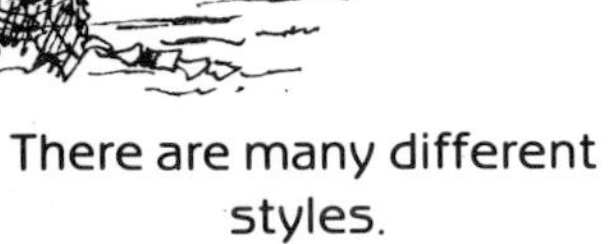

There are many different styles.

PLANES AND ROCKETS

Sometimes 'space' cannot be left without the artist exploring things that should fit there.

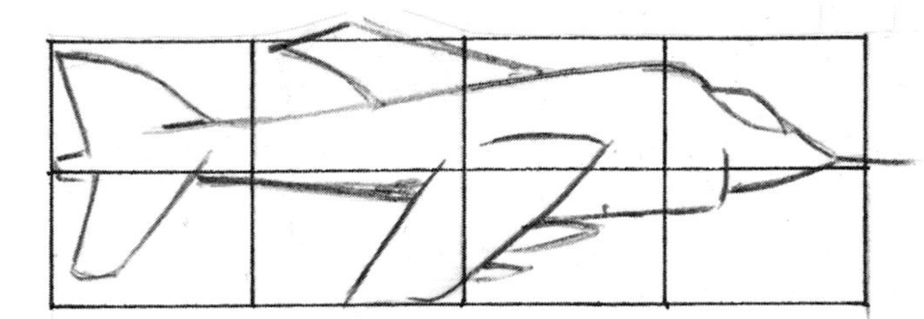

Now you probably think that everything starts with a rectangle!

Get the sweep shape first

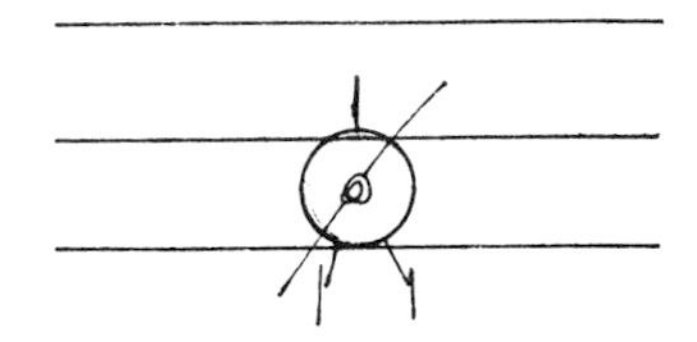

Look what you can do with a circle and some lines.

Start with a cross.

A cigar shape.

Keep lines clear and crisp!

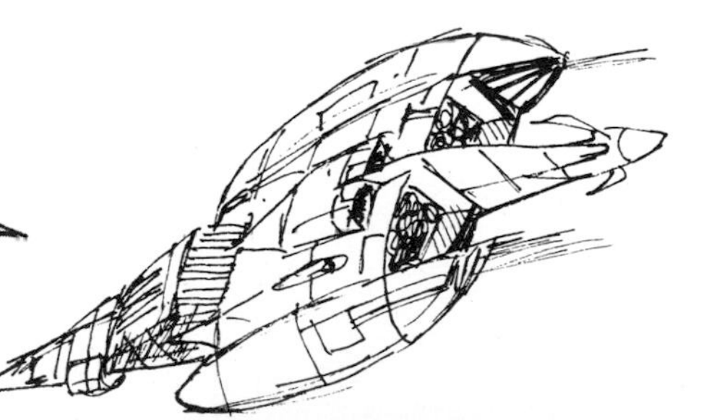

Use models and toys as your subjects. Build an illustrated story with your pictures.

CARTOONS

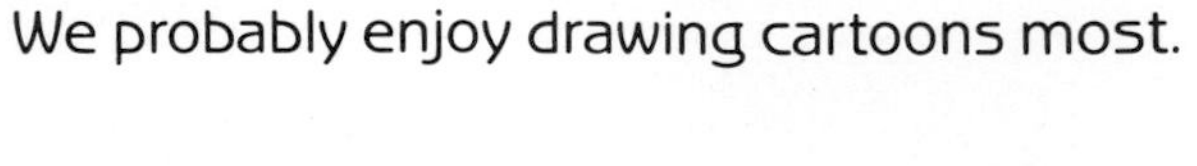

We probably enjoy drawing cartoons most.

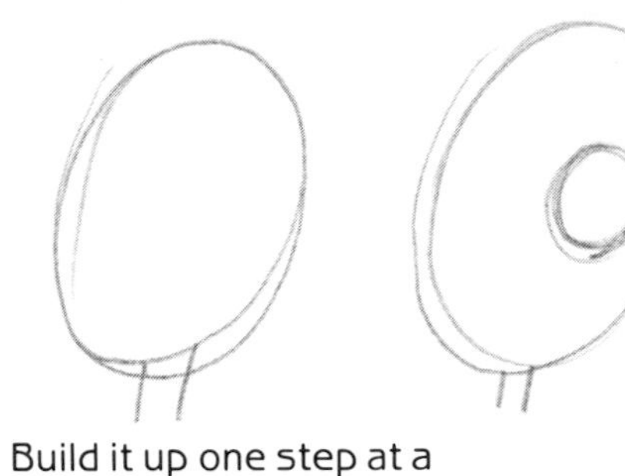

Build it up one step at a time.

A quick cartoon face – a circle and four dots. Add to this beginning.

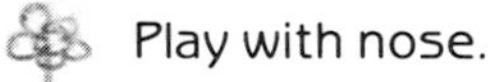

Open mouth – closed eyes.

Play with nose.

Change shape.

Profile.

Play with nose and mouth.

Don't forget hair, hat or glasses.

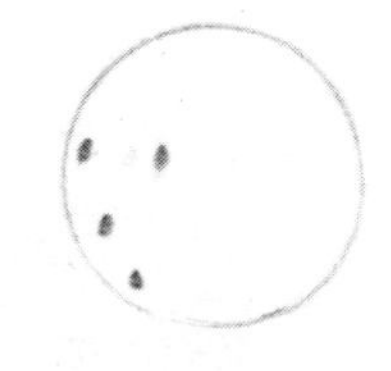
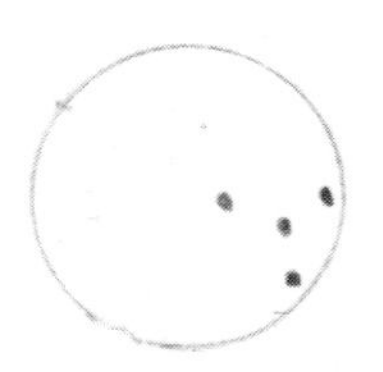

Direction.

Some examples that began with just four dots.

Experiment with features – exaggerate! Different expressions and angles are good practice!

CARTOONS AGAIN

Making a figure from sausage shapes.

Making a triangle figure.

Cartooning on bend.

Built for speed.

Everything in cartoons is simple and/or exaggerated.

Draw a funny picture to show a happening you've seen this week.

CARICATURES

A caricature is a technique where we exaggerate a person's looks to make a cartoon figure.

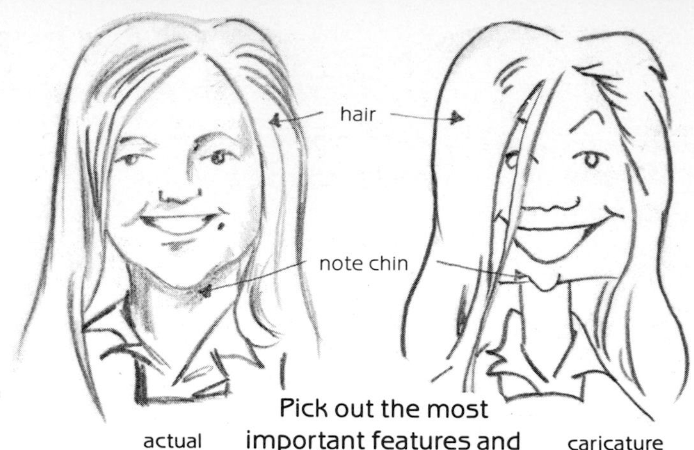

Pick out the most important features and exaggerate them.

Look for the basic shape of the face.

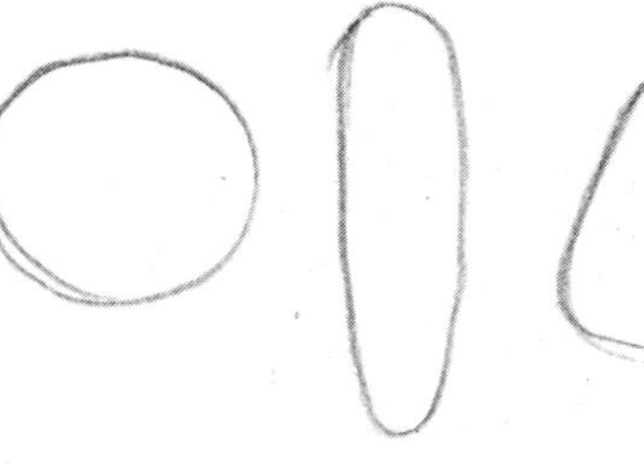

Omit or minimise points to help emphasise.

Add hair style (this helps to tell who it is – so take your time).

Try to draw as little as possible, then see if you can recognise the person.

Add detail – start with what you see as the main feature (big nose, glasses, big eyes, lips, missing teeth).

Where do you see caricatures used? Make a collection. Try to do your family or friends as caricatures. See if others know who it is.

MONSTERS AND OTHER THINGS

Now we can really start to play around with our lines ... models may be a problem, however!

A shapely start.

Directional lines start.

A few lines plot the size and shape.

Collect pictures of creatures from magazines, then make your own book of weird monsters.

YOUR OWN STYLE — IMAGINATION

Because it needs no preparation, you can practise drawing most anywhere — using any subject or just a touch of memory and a vivid imagination.

AND I THOUGHT ALL ABSTRACTS WERE PAINTED!

Draw unusual pictures using a particular style.

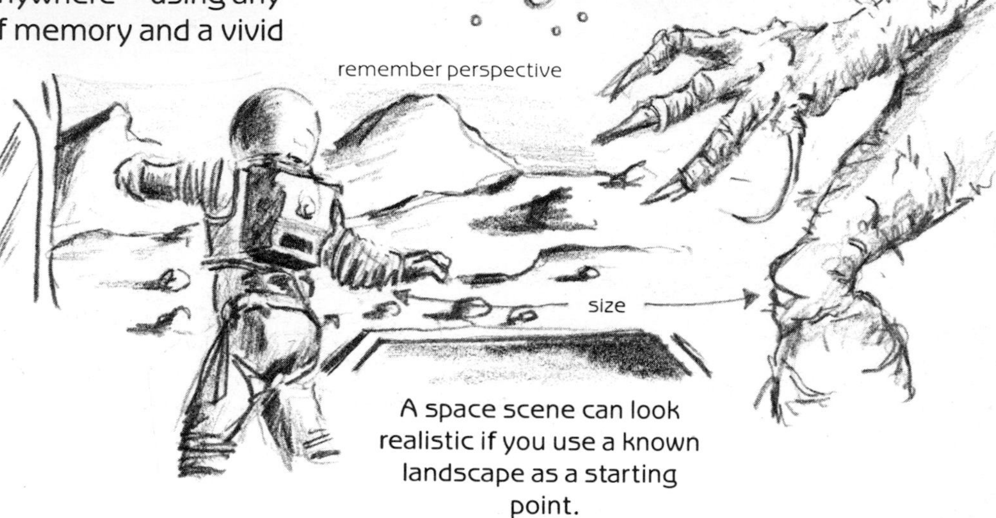

A space scene can look realistic if you use a known landscape as a starting point.

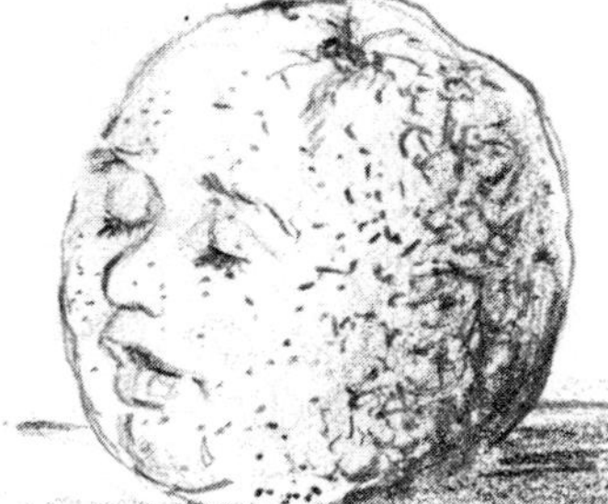

Combine two subjects into one drawing.

You can make a really strange picture by deliberately mixing your rules on size and overlapping.

What about making an abstract by looking through holes?

Now put down the book and get to it. Draw! Anywhere, anytime, anyway!